CONTEMPORARY
SCIENCE FICTION, FANTASY,
AND
HORROR POETRY

Contemporary
Science Fiction, Fantasy,
and
Horror Poetry

A RESOURCE GUIDE
AND BIOGRAPHICAL
DIRECTORY

Scott E. Green

GREENWOOD PRESS
New York • Westport, Connecticut • London

Library of Congress Cataloging-in-Publication Data

Green, Scott E.
    Contemporary science fiction, fantasy, and horror poetry : a
resource guide and biographical directory / Scott E. Green.
        p.   cm.
    Includes indexes.
    ISBN 0-313-26324-8 (lib. bdg. : alk. paper)
    1. Fantastic poetry, American—Indexes. 2. American poetry—
20th century—Indexes. 3. Fantastic poetry, American—Bio-
bibliography. 4. Poets, American—20th century—Biography—
Directories. 5. American periodicals—Indexes. 6. Fantastic poetry,
English—Indexes. 7. English poetry—20th century—Indexes. 8.
Fantastic poetry, English—Bio-bibliography. 9. Poets, English—
20th century—Biography—Directories. I. Title
Z1231.Q7G74   1989
[PS309.F35]
016.811'50801—dc20   89-16966

British Library Cataloguing in Publication Data is available.

Library of Congress Catalog Card Number: 89-16966
ISBN: 0-313-26324-8

First published in 1989

Greenwood Press, Inc.
88 Post Road West, Westport, Connecticut 06881

Printed in the United States of America

The paper used in this book complies with the
Permanent Paper Standard issued by the National
Information Standards Organization (Z39.48–1984).

10 9 8 7 6 5 4 3 2 1

This work is dedicated to four people:

My mother, who typed and then retyped the whole manuscript

My father, who carefully supervised her

Dr. Suzette H. Elgin, who bought my very first poem and got me started

Dr. James Gunn, who got me thinking about doing a reference work in
this field.

Contents

Preface

This book seeks to document a basic proposition: that poetry is a major form of expression for writers of science fiction, fantasy, and horror. It further provides evidence that there *are* opportunities for publishing such genre poetry. Included in the volume are guides to major magazines that publish such poetry — both commercial and small-press magazines — each with an index of poets published; a bibliography of major anthologies with the poetry listed; and a biographical directory of poets active in the three genres. An appendix of awards, a general index, and an index of poem titles complete the work.

The three main sections — on magazines, anthologies, and poets — are intended to give the reader a sense of the roots and current trends in science fiction, fantasy, and horror poetry. The book is not a history of poetry in the three genres or a manual on poetry writing; however, the introductory section offers a brief overview of science fiction, fantasy, and horror poetry publishing in the United States.

The focus of the work is on American writers who publish in America, though foreign writers and publications, especially British, are also included because there have always been considerable interrelationships among American and British writers and publications. Further, both British writers and British magazines have played an important role in the evolution of poetry in American science fiction, fantasy, and horror literature. Both commercial and small-press outlets are explored, but fanzines, the amateur publications of the unique subculture known as fandom, are for the most part beyond the scope of this book.

Science fiction, fantasy, and horror are considered primarily as distinct genres in American literature. However, some of the poets included write in the genres for mainstream markets and have little or no contact with the distinctly genre publications. While science fiction, fantasy, and horror are all distinct forms of literature, they remain subsets of the literature of the fantastic. Few poets can be described as purely science fiction, fantasy, or horror poets. Many readily cross the borders of all three forms as well as that of the surreal and speculative. Others in this work can only be described as sui generis.

These three categories of poetry — horror, fantasy, and science fiction — for the most part will be considered collectively in this volume. However, some differentiation is in order. The first two categories are probably already defined in the minds of most readers. Horror poetry is simply poetry that describes or conveys a sense of horror to the reader. The source of horror in the poem need not be of supernatural or fantastic origin. Fantasy poems are based on mythic or folkloric themes. They may be broadly described as presupposing that magical and supernatural phenomena exist. Under this definition, surreal poems, magic reality poems, and any poem that does not accept the physical universe may be included in this category. Fantasy poems are frequently written in traditional forms and are generally narrative. The poems are usually set in a universe where magic and supernatural creatures abound, though these two elements may not be immediately evident.

Some horror poems may be described as fantasy poems. What makes a fantasy poem also a horror poem depends on the intent. If the poem seeks to convey a sense of horror and fear to the reader, then it is a horror poem. There are poems that may have elements of both horror and fantasy but are lighthearted and humorous. These poems, equivalent to prose referred to as light or mainstream fantasy, have themes that may be familiar to viewers of films and television adaptions such as "Topper," "The Ghost and Mrs. Muir," or "I Dream of Jeannie."

Problems of definition arise in what constitutes a science fiction poem. The simplest answer would be any poem that is published in a science fiction magazine or anthology, but more precise definitions are needed. Suzette H. Elgin, a noted science fiction novelist and poet, defined a science fiction poem as having "a narrative component and a science component." This is a definition that she has frequently used in telephone conversations with me and in the pages of *Star*Line*, the newsletter of the Science Fiction Poetry Association. Elgin never elaborated upon this definition. However, it seems to be a useful stepping-off point for others attempting to define science fiction poetry.

While a single definition still evades us, four distinct classes of published poems can be discerned:

1. The *science fiction narrative poem* is any poem that tells a story, frequently using the conventions associated with science fiction literature, such as time travel, planetary exploration, and human/alien communications.
2. *Poems of science* are poems that speak about scientific phenomena, the lives of scientists and the relationship of science and society. These poems frequently find markets outside of genre publications, especially in Britain.
3. *Poems of commentary* are poems that critique or comment upon themes in science fiction literature and film rather than narrating a story.
4. *Speculative poems* relate themes associated with science fiction such as time travel and interstellar exploration but use language and structure associated with mainstream poetry. They are often written by mainstream poets and appear in mainstream publications. Their primary concern is the human condition, not adherence to traditional science fiction plots. Certain fantasy and horror poems also fall under this definition.

Notwithstanding, a poem may embrace one or more of the above definitions.

Information in this book came from three main sources. The first was correspondence and telephone conversations between the author and various poets, writers, and organizations, including *Aboriginal SF,* Duane Ackerson, Brian Aldiss, Dick Allen, *Amazing,* Poul Anderson, Isaac Asimov, Elspeth Aubrey, Lee Ballentine, Ruth Berman, George Bessette, John G. Betancourt, *Beyond,* Sue C. Bever, Michael Bishop, Harry Bose, Bruce Boston, Joseph P. Brennan, Reginald Bretnor, Mrs. John Brunner, Cathy Buburuz, David Bunch, Sandra S. Burkhardt, Lee Burwasser, Jack Butler, Dave Calder, Lin Carter, Mary E. Choo, Prof. Joe R. Christopher, Mitchell Cohen, Valerie Nieman Colander, Michael R. Collins, S. R. Compton, H. J. Cording, Dan Crawford, Gary Crawford, Annette S. Crouch, Jo Anna Dale, Keith Allen Daniels, L. Sprague de Camp, Charles de Lint, John Devin, Tom Disch, C. Clark Donaldson, Jr., James S. Dorr, Yael Dragwyla, Denise Dumars, Patricia C. Dunn, Roger Dutcher, George Alec Effinger, Thomas M. Egan, Stephen Eng, Jody Forest, Janet Fox, Robert Frazier, Esther Friesner, Joey Froehlich, Terry Garey, John Francis Haines, Joe Haldeman,

Haunts, Dwight E. Humphries, *Infinity Skewed*, *Isaac Asimov Science Fiction Magazine*, Ken Johnson, Andrew Joron, Scott A. Kelly, Millea Kenin, Eileen Kernaghan, Virginia Kidd, David Kopaska-Merkel, Mercedes R. Lackey, James A. Lee, Esther M. Leiper, Lisa Lepovetsky, A. M. Lightner, Alun Llewellyn, David Lunde, Jack Lundy, F. Gwynplaine MacIntyre, Ron Maggiano, Elissa Malcohn, Adrianne Marcus, Sue Marra, Frederick J. Mayer, Ardath Mayhar, Judith Moffett, Edwin Morgan, A. R. Morlan, Sam Moskowitz, Edward Mycue, Off-Centaur Publications, Ocean View Books, Susan Palwick, Peter Payack, Marthyan Pelegrimas, Ace Pilkington, Jonathan Post, Kathryn Rantala, Wendy Rathbone, Melanie A. Rawls, Jonathan Raz, Thomas A. Rentz, Jr., Mark Rich, Tom Riley, Prof. John B. Rosenman, Mr. and Mrs. Chuck Rothman, Brett Rutherford, Wayne Allen Sallee, Debra F. Sanders, Marlene Y. Satter, Lorraine Schein, Ann K. Schwader, Darrell Schweitzer, Science Fiction Poetry Association, Ian Shires, Donald Sidney-Fryer, Marge Simon, John Sladek, Small Press Writers and Artists Organization, Steve Sneyd, *Space & Time*, Douglas Spangle, Nancy Springer, David Starkey, Sephanie Stearns, Chris Stevenson, W. Gregory Stewart, Michael Stiles, Del Stone, Jr., Steve Rasnic Tem, Teratara Publications, Terminus Publications, Frederick Turner, *2 AM*, Jim Van Pelt, Ralph E. Vaughan, Lyn Venable, Charles West, Thomas Wiloch, Billy Wolfenbarger, Jane Yolen, Ree Young, George Zebrowski, Roger Zelazny and *Z Miscellaneous*.

The second principal source was *Star*Line* (1977–1988, presently located at Elissa Malcohn's address). Every issue had data relevant to this book. The third principal source of data was the introductory and biographical notes found in the following anthologies: *Aliens & Lovers*, *Burning with a Vision*, *Elsewhere*, *Holding Your Eight Hands*, *Operation: Phantasy*, *Poly*, *Songs from Unsung Worlds*, and *The Umbral Anthology of Science Fiction Poetry*. The anthologies cited were carefully read as were most issues of every magazine title listed.

Acknowledgments

I should like to thank my parents for their support of me in this project. Thanks are also due to Dr. James Gunn, Elaine Bloom, and Sharlene E. Gilman, who in different ways inspired me to do this book.

The assistance of the M.I.T. Science Fiction Society, its members (particularly Ken Johnson), and its library was essential to the research needed for this book, and I gratefully acknowledge it.

Finally, I must thank all the writers, editors, and publishers for their responses to my letters and telephone calls. In particular, I should like to thank Lee Ballentine, Bruce Boston, David Bunch, Michael Collings, Janet Fox, Elissa Malcohn, Jonathan Post, and George Zebrowski for their comments.

Introduction: A Brief History of Science Fiction, Fantasy, and Horror Poetry Publishing in America

Themes from science fiction, fantasy, and horror have always been an intimate part of mainstream poetry in the United States and abroad. However, the publishing of poetry by those American writers who embraced science fiction, fantasy, and horror as unique genres with values that set them apart from the rest of fiction has been less common and traditionally had only limited and unpublicized appearances in genre publications. Nevertheless, poetry has been a part of the genres from the very beginning of their development. Both *Weird Tales* and *Amazing* have published poetry since their founding. Poetry was always there as an equal part of these magazines, though poems were often used as fillers and frequently not listed in the table of contents. In this respect there was no difference from the treatment of poetry of any type in mainstream publications.

Throughout the 1920s, 1930s, and 1940s pulp magazines in all three genres printed poetry. The only major exception was *Astounding* under the editorship of John Campbell, Jr. Campbell could never bring himself to buy poetry for his magazine, though ironically he did buy poetry for *Unknown*, *Astounding*'s fantasy-oriented sister magazine. In contrast the various editors at *Weird Tales* featured poetry by their major contributors such as H. P. Lovecraft, Robert E. Howard, and Clark Ashton Smith. After World War II the nature of genre publishing changed. The large pulp magazines shrank to digest size, which was considered an up-to-date look. Many magazine editors in the field wanted to emulate the editorial tone and voice of Campbell's *Astounding*. The no-nonsense hard science fiction that it featured became an important nodel for other editors and writers. Part of their up-to-date look was the absence of poetry from the magazine pages.

A second editorial voice was set by H. L. Gold and his new science fiction magazine *Galaxy*. *Galaxy* was a showcase for satirical science fiction. It did not publish poetry either, probably for the same reason that *Astounding* had rejected it. Poetry somehow was a part of the old pulpish tradition that Gold sought to discard.

Poetry persisted in two very different kinds of magazines. The first was science fiction and fantasy horror magazines whose editorial tastes and standards had been set in the pulpish era of the 1930s and 1940s. Some of these magazines, *Fantastic Universe* among them, were post–World War II in origin, but their tastes were frozen in a 1938 time warp. The other showcase for poetry in the three genres was *The Magazine of Fantasy and Science Fiction*. Since its beginning in 1949, its editorial policy has been to elevate the literary standards of science fiction, fantasy, and horror. It had no editorial prejudice against poetry, and throughout the 1950s and 1960s it and the various reprint anthologies it generated were the principal market for poetry.

Despite these bright spots, magazines for genre writers started a long decline after World War II. Their place was taken by the paperback original and the hardbound reprint. Only Arkham House, the specialized publisher of fantasy, horror, and occasional science fiction, regularly published collections of poetry by major horror writers such as Lovecraft.

There was a change during the 1960s. New important showcases started to elevate the status of poetry in commercial genre science fiction. First, Judith Merrrill in 1958 began including poetry in her year's best science fiction anthology. Much of this poetry came from outside the traditional science fiction publications. Second was the evolution of the British science fiction magazine *New Worlds* from a rather tired version of *Analog* to a magazine with a specific purpose. It emphasized the importance of literary value over traditional science fiction themes in its pages and chose to become the showcase where writers speculating about the future of people and society would be published. Many British and some American poets, such as Peter Redgrove and Tom Disch, found that their poetry was valued as strongly as their prose. This work, collectively referred to as "New Wave," also started to appear in Merrill's anthologies. Third, there were numerous attempts to start newsstand horror magazines, most of which reprinted considerable poetry from *Weird Tales*. This was not surprising, since the editor of most of these efforts was Robert Lowdnes, an old editorial hand from the pulp era and a poet in his own right.

Horror and fantasy fans were being reintroduced to the tradition of poetry within their favorite genre.

As the 1960s progressed, two things happened. Many writers entering the field of science fiction and fantasy had strong academic backgrounds in literature and writing and were used to working with poetry. Further, numerous original science fiction and fantasy anthologies appeared by individuals who also had strong literary backgrounds and had no problems recognizing the appropriateness of poetry. Not every anthology had poetry, but neither was it a rarity. The boom in original anthologies started to play out by 1976. Yet it had served an important purpose: It revived an interest in poetry among genre science fiction, fantasy, and horror writers.

This rekindled interest has determined the present status of poetry in contemporary science fiction, fantasy, and horror. A significant event was the creation of the Science Fiction Poetry Association in 1977 by Suzette Elgin and others to promote an interest in poetry in all three genres, not just science fiction. This association has played a major role in promoting poetry to professional editors. It also helped establish programming on poetry at science fiction conventions. Its newsletter, *Star*Line,* became a forum for science fiction, fantasy, and horror poets. The group became the voice of genre poetry.

The year 1977 also saw the founding of the *Isaac Asimov Science Fiction Magazine.* Under the editorship of George Scithers, it became a major showcase for poetry. A revitalized *Amazing* soon joined it in buying poetry. Ironically, at the same time the *Magazine of Fantasy and Science Fiction* started to reduce the number of poems it was publishing. Scithers also illustrates another important trend that revitalized poetry in American genre markets beginning in the 1970s. He is one of many editors who publish and edit small-press science fiction, fantasy, and horror magazines. His magazine, *Amra,* which is dedicated to sword and sorcery fiction and poetry, was one of the first such small-press publications. By 1977, *Amra* had been joined by others such as *Space & Time, Eternity, Owlflight, Pandora,* and *Whispers.* These magazines evolved because newsstand publications for short fiction were fast dwindling. Many small-press magazines purchased their material but at less than commercial rates.

Most of the editors of these publications have a strong literary background and are as comfortable with poetry as they are with prose. Many are poets in their own right. As in the mainstream small press, poetry prospers in genre small press.

Today, poetry has become a permanent part of genre fiction in America. It has at least two permanent newsstand magazine publications, *Isaac Asimov* and *Amazing*. There is a strong and vigorous small-press for genre poetry. Genre poetry has its own awards, the Rhyslings. Poets can become full members of the Science Fiction Writers of America, the leading professional group in the genre, just on the strength of their poetry sales.

The status of poetry in American genre science fiction, fantasy, and horror is more secure. Nevertheless, much still has to be done before a poet can say, "Yes, I am a poet and I am a science fiction writer, a fantasy writer, a horror writer," and not be looked upon as an oddity.

I.
Poetry in Magazines

Commercial and Newsstand Genre Magazines

The newsstand magazine has been the core of American science fiction, fantasy, and horror since the inception of the pulp magazines after World War I. *Weird Tales* in all its incarnations always had poetry. As mentioned earlier, the other genre pulp magazines, except for *Astounding*, regularly published poetry of all lengths.

Today, newsstand magazines play a less visible role in modern American science fiction, fantasy, and horror. Yet, they remain important. First, they are the most important publications for fiction by new writers as well as the only ongoing major ones for short fiction. Second, their nonfiction columns and editorials frequently determine the shape and form of the genres. Finally, whatever the magazines publish legitimizes new innovative approaches within the three genres. The fact that poetry appears on a regular basis in *Amazing* and *Isaac Asimov* tells the reader in the field that poetry is a legitimate form of expression.

Listed below are nineteen commercial science fiction, fantasy, and horror magazines that have regularly used poetry since 1949, when *The Magazine of Fantasy and Science Fiction*, the first postwar science fiction magazine to have a regular policy of buying poetry, began. Included under each entry is an alphabetical list of poets who have appeared in each magazine with issue information. Unless otherwise noted, individual issues are identified by month and year.

Not listed are magazines that do not normally publish poetry including *Analog*, *Omni*, and *Twilight Zone*. *Analog* throughout its entire history, beginning as *Astounding* and currently, has published only two pieces of poetry. Both times its readership responded so negatively to the poems that the editors promised never to use poetry again. However, in the past two years that policy has changed, and poetry has been published by *Analog*. *Omni* claims that it never publishes poetry. The one time that a poem (Joe Haldeman's "Saul's Death") did appear in its pages, it was listed as a short story. *Twilight Zone* also claimed that it did not publish poetry, but poetry did appear on its pages before its demise. Perhaps it may be safer to say that the magazine occasionally solicited poems but it did not accept unsolicited poetry manuscripts. *Weird Tales* is included for its issues appearing since the early 1970s. The magazine had a continuous unbroken existence from 1923 to 1954; however, the original *Weird Tales* print run is not covered because the focus of this book is on the postwar and contemporary period.

All the titles that I have covered are American with the exception of the British *New Worlds*, which certainly influenced the growth of poetry in American science fiction. Poetry does regularly appear in many foreign science fiction magazines. The recently deceased Australian magazine *Void* published poetry even though its editors stoutly maintained that they did not have a poetry publication policy. Oddly enough, the only major surviving British science fiction magazine, *Interzone*, does not use poetry even though in every other respect it emulates *New Worlds*.

Following the nineteen magazine listings is a roster of poets who have appeared in other commercial and newsstand genre magazines.

Aboriginal SF

Founded in 1986, *Aboriginal SF* tends toward hard adventure science fiction. Currently in a tabloid form, the magazine does not have regular newsstand distribution. Its editorial policy toward poetry reflects a similar taste as its prose. Light, but not necessarily humorous, pieces with hard science fiction themes are its specialty. The numbers listed refer to sequence of release, not dates.

Bruce Boston: #7	David Lunde: #2
Robert Frazier: #2	Elissa Malcohn: #9
Bonita Kale: #9	Wendy Rathbone: #6
Peg Livertus: #3	

Amazing

Amazing has been one of the two leading magazine markets for science fiction and fantasy poetry since 1980. Before 1980 it did publish an occasional poem after World War II as did its sister magazine *Fantastic*. However, the poets listed below date from the time when the magazine, under the editorship of Elinor Mavor, started to use poetry as a regular policy. Now owned by TSR, Inc., it is edited by Pat Price, who has a preference for poems that spoof traditional science fiction and fantasy clichés. Price also has a taste for poems about readers' reactions to science fiction and fantasy. Of course, there are more serious poems published in its pages, but the thrust of both the poetry and prose is toward a sense of fun and pleasure. For some reason *Amazing* has had more poets make their first appearance in its pages than has *Isaac Asimov*, the other leading science fiction market.

Buck Allen: 1/88
Arlan Andrews: 7/88
Elton Andrews: 11/87
M. Ann Arkee: 3/87
Hope Athearn: 3/83, 3/84
Benedict Auer: 7/87, 3/88
Jim Barnes: 11/80
Greg Benford: 11/81
Ruth Berman: 7/86, 3/88
John Betancourt: 1/84, 7/85,
    11/85
Bruce Boston: 3/87, 5/87, 7/87,
    1/88, 5/88, 7/88
Anthony J. Bryant: 3/88
David R. Bunch: 1/81, 5/81, 7/81,
    9/81, 11/81
Orson Scott Card: 11/81
Joe-Bob Carothers: 11/86
Ellin Carter: 3/82, 11/82, 1/83,
    5/84
Lawrence C. Connolly: 3/82
Wil Creveling: 7/84, 3/85
Lorna Crowe: 7/85
Mike Curry: 5/87, 9/87, 1/88,
    3/88, 7/88
Paul Dellinger: 6/82
Mike M. DeSimone: 3/82
John Devin: 1/85, 5/85, 3/86,
    5/86, 7/86, 1/87, 3/87, 5/87,
    7/87, 5/88

Thomas M. Disch: 3/83, 5/83,
    7/84, 3/85, 7/85, 9/85, 11/85,
    3/86, 5/86, 5/87
Roger Dutcher: 1/84
Scott Edelman: 7/81
Stephen Eng: 7/84
John M. Ford: 7/84, 11/84,
    1/85
Robert Frazier: 9/81, 11/81, 6/82,
    9/83, 1/84, 9/84, 9/86, 11/86,
    1/87, 3/87, 9/87, 11/87, 1/88
Tim Friel: 1/83
Esther M. Friesner: 11/85, 1/86,
    9/86, 5/88, 7/88
Joey Froehlich: 7/81, 11/81, 3/82,
    9/84
Felix Gottschalk: 9/81
Beverly Grant: 1/85
Scott E. Green: 3/81, 7/81, 3/82,
    9/82
Robert Hays: 11/87
Jack R. Hill: 9/87
Kenneth Hill: 9/85
Robert E. Howard: 1/85, 3/86
Shelton Arnel Johnson: 3/87,
    11/87
Andrew Joron: 9/81, 6/82, 11/82,
    1/84, 11/86, 9/87
Marvin Kaye: 1/81, 5/81
Thomas Kearney: 7/86

Christopher Brown Kelly: 3/86
James Patrick Kelly: 9/82
S. A. Kelly: 11/87
Arthur L. Klein: 1/87, 3/87, 7/87
Scott Koeller: 11/85
Erwin Krieger: 11/81
Everett Lee Lady: 11/84
David Langford: 7/85
Sharon Lee: 9/81
Morris Liebson: 7/86, 11/86, 9/87, 5/88
F. Gwyplaine MacIntyre: 3/83, 7/83, 1/85, 3/85, 11/85, 1/86, 9/86, 11/87
Elissa Malcohn: 1/88
Ted Mancuso: 9/82
Edward Martindale: 3/82, 11/82
Steven Edward McDonald: 3/81, 5/81
Wendy McElroy: 3/83, 9/83, 9/84, 1/85
Robert R. Medcalf: 6/82
Steve Miller: 9/81
Ron Montana: 3/82
L. A. P. Moore: 1/81
Susan Heyboen O'Keefe: 5/84
Susan Palwick: 1/85, 7/85, 5/86

Peter Payack: 9/81, 11/81, 11/82, 11/84
Ace G. Pilkington: 7/86, 5/87, 7/87, 11/87, 7/88
Frederick Pohl: 5/88
Christine Post: 5/88
Jonathan Post: 5/88
Shari Prange: 9/81
Mark Rich: 1/87
Ruth Lisa Schechter: 11/83
Darrell Schweitzer: 5/80, 6/82, 1/86, 5/86, 7/86, 9/87
John D. Seats: 6/82, 9/82
William Shakespeare: 5/86
Margaret B. Simon: 7/87
Chris Harold Stevenson: 5/88, 7/88
Michael Stiles: 7/88
Steven Rasnic Tem: 3/81
Frederick Turner: 5/85
Steven M. Tymon: 11/82
Kurt von Stuckrad: 3/81
K. C. Warren: 3/88
William Jon Watkins: 7/87
Richard Wilson: 9/86, 5/87, 9/87
Michael A. Winters: 7/86
Gene Wolfe: 1/85, 3/86
Roger Zelazny: 7/81

Ariel

Ariel was a very expensive short-lived, glossy-sized science fiction magazine that was published from 1976 to 1977. The few poems that appeared in it were mostly reprints. It was more concerned with art portfolios than either prose or poetry. The numbers listed refer to sequence, not to dates.

Ray Bradbury: #4
Robert E. Howard: #2

Edgar Allan Poe: #2
Roger Zelazany: #2

Asimov Science Fiction Adventure Magazine

A short-lived, glossy-sized companion magazine to *Isaac Asimov Science Fiction Magazine*, its short life was one more proof that a glossy-sized science fiction magazine would always have problems surviving on the newsstand. As its title implies, both its prose and poetry focused on adventure science fiction. It flourished in 1978 and 1979.

Randall Garrett: Spring 1979   Ray Russell: Fall 1978

Coven 13

A digest-sized horror magazine, *Coven 13* attempted to be a magazine in the *Weird Tales* tradition and soon disappeared like any victim of a *Weird Tales* short story. It was published in 1969 and 1970 by Marvel Comics.

Robert E. Howard: 3/70   Manly Wade Wellman: 1/70
Walden Muss: 9/69, 10/69

Fantastic

Fantastic was a fantasy magazine companion to *Amazing*, existing during the 1940s, 1950s, 1960s, and 1970s. At the start of Elinor Mavor's editorship, it persisted for a while before being merged into *Amazing*.

Frank C. Gunderloy: 4/80   Steven Rasnic Tem: 1/80
Kurt von Stuckard: 10/79

Fantasy Book

Fantasy Book was a glossy-sized magazine devoted to high fantasy and some horror. While a professional magazine in every respect, it never sought newsstand distribution per se. Most of its poetry was light rhymed and metered pieces that gave a slightly skewed vision of high and heroic fantasy. This was one of the publications in which poets who previously had established a reputation in small-press and fannish outlets had their first major appearance. Its owners temporarily suspended the magazine in 1987, so that they could focus their energies establishing an independent comic book line, Hero Comics. They are now planning to start up *Fantasy Book* once again. *Fantasy Book* is not to be confused with a magazine of the same name which appeared in the late 1940s. The magazine was founded in 1981.

Lee Adkins: 9/85
Arlan Andrews: 3/87
Lee Barwood (pseud. for Marlene
    Y. Satter) 11/82
Theodore R. Cogswell: 5/83
Michael Collings: 6/85
Mary Elizabeth Counselman:
    3/85
Marilyn Crane: 3/84
John Edward Damon: 3/85
Harry Davidov: 6/86
James S. Dorr: 6/86
Denise Dumars: 2/83
Mary Alice Fox: 6/84
Robert Frazier: 11/82, 6/84,
    9/85,12/85
Esther Friesner: 9/84, 9/85, 12/85
Joel Hagen: 2/82
Robert E. Howard: 9/84, 9/86,

3/87
Mercedes Lackey: 3/86
Sharon Lee: 5/82
Magenta Marguette: 12/83
Ardath Mayhar: 6/85, 9/86
Jim Neal: 12/81, 5/82, 5/83,
    12/83, 12/85, 9/86
Attanielle Annyn Noel: 5/83
Lee Nordling: 12/83
Jonathan V. Post: 8/83
Jean Poynter: 3/84
Darrell Schweitzer: 12/86
Nancy Springer: 2/82, 11/82,
    12/83
Karen G. Trimble: 8/82
Leilah Wendell: 12/81
t. Winter-Damon: 3/87
Jane Yolen: 3/87

Forgotten Fantasy

This magazine reprinted fantasy from the nineteenth century.

Thomas Lovell Beddoes: 10/70
Richard LeGailienne: 6/71

Matthew Gregory Lewis: 12/70

Galileo

Galileo was a glossy-sized science fiction magazine that flourished from 1976 to 1981. While it lasted longer than most, its publishers folded because of legal problems concerning attempts to get newsstand distribution. Toward the end of its existence, its publishers purchased a moribund *Galaxy* and came out with one issue in 1980 that had a Bob Frazier poem. *Galileo* purchased prose and poetry that centered around ideas rather than conflicts. One of its publishers, Charles Ryan, started *Aboriginal SF*.

Diane Ackerman: #2
Ray Bradbury: #3, #7

Peter Dillingham: #5
Roy Lichtenstein: #10

Isaac Asimov Science Fiction Magazine

Starting in 1978, *Isaac Asimov Science Fiction Magazine* was the second postwar science fiction or fantasy magazine that regularly published poetry that still operates to this day. Under its first editor, George Scithers, *Isaac Asimov* used poetry that tended to be light, humorous, and heavily structured, in other words the kind of poetry that frequently appears in science fiction fanzines. This is not surprising, since Scithers is an old-time fan and has edited his fair share of fanzines and small-press magazines. Under its current editor, Gardner Dozois, the poetry has tended to become more serious and introspective, though Dozois does share Scithers's taste for meter and rhyme. It also seems that fewer poets are appearing in its pages.

Don Anderson: 6/81, 8/82, 10/82,
  2/83, 11/83
Poul Anderson: 9/80, 10/80
Arlan Keith Andrews, Sr.: 1/80
Fan D. Ango: 1/80
Ron Antonucci: 4/83
Argus: 5/80
Isaac Asimov: Fall 77, 7/82
Hope Athearn: 3/81, 12/82, 7/83,
  7/84, 2/85, 8/86
Gregory Benford: 12/86
Don R. Benson: Winter 77
Ruth Berman: Fall 77
Michael Bishop: 9/84, 1/85
Bernard Blicksilver: 3/82, 12/83
Bruce Boston: 9/83, 4/84, 12/84,
  5/85, 9/85, 12/86, 1/87, 8/87,
  5/88
Will Briggs: 2/82
Mike Buckley: 3/80
David Bunch: 1/81, 4/82, 8/82,
  3/85, 10/85
Brad Calhoon: 3/79
Grant Carrington: 3/80
Vic Compton: 8/80

S. Dale: Winter 77, 5/78, 2/80
Keith Davis: 2/79
John DeCamp: 4/84
Bradley Denton: 8/85
Ken Duff: 11/80
Roger Dutcher: 2/83, 12/83, 5/86,
  9/87, 10/87, 4/88
Suzette H. Elgin: 10/85, 12/85
Norah Falstein: 7/82
Max Fell: 5/82
Julie Flores: 5/79
John M. Ford: 5/78, 7/78, 11/78,
  3/80
Robert Frazier: 11/79, 8/80, 2/81,
  8/81, 2/82, 3/82, 4/82, 5/82,
  9/82, 11/82, 12/ 82, 1/83,
  3/83, 4/83, 6/83, 8/83, 12/83,
  7/84, 12/84, 2/85, 5/85, 8/85,
  11/85, 12/85, 1/86, 6/86,
  8/86, 10/86, 12/86, 2/87,
  3/87, 4/87, 5/87, 6/87, 7/87,
  8/87, 10/87, 2/88
Donald Gaither: 5/78
Randall Garrett: 9/78, 1/82
Darcy Giene: 3/80

Norma Gjuka: 6/83
Beverly Grant: 3/81, 10/81, 11/82
Mark Grenier: 1/78, 11/78
Jeffrey Haas: 5/78
Joe Haldeman: 12/86, 12/87
Elissa L. A. Hamilton (earlier pseud. for E. Malcohn): Mid-Dec./83
Dan J. Hicks: 7/79
Kenneth Hill: 4/86
Charles J. Hoist: 10/81
Bryan A. Hollerbach: 2/82, 5/82
Carl Holzman: 8/80
Akua Lezli Hope: 4/85
Jeanne Hopkins: 9/79
Seth S. Horowitz: 3/78
J. J. Hunt: 9/87
M. G. Jacobs: 3/83
Alex M. Jeffers: 4/85, 6/86
Anne Devereaux Jordan: 2/83, 12/86
Andrew Joron: 9/82, 5/85, 11/85
Wayne A. Kallunki: 7/83
Thomas Kearney: 4/86, 6/86
Julia Keller: 11/78
Lee Killough: 6/83
Andrew Klavan: 5/88
Marc Laidlaw: 10/86
Stephanie Lang: 10/79
D. C. Lewis: 2/81
Barry Longyear: 10/79
David Lunde: 4/84, 2/86
F. Gwynplaine MacIntyre: 7/80, 11/80, 1/81, 2/81, 4/81, 5/81, 6/81, 7/81, 8/81, 9/81, 10/81, 11/81, 2/82, 6/82, 2/83, 9/83
Claire Mahan: 12/80
S. Scott Matulis: 9/81
Roger Meador: 1/86
Catherine Mintz: 3/83
M. L. Nelson: 7/85

William E. Nilsen: 8/81, 1/82
Peggy J. Noonan: 4/81
Jon P. Ogden: 10/81
Sally Palmer: 4/80
Susan Palwick: 6/85, 9/85, 3/86
Peter Payack: 4/79, 7/79, 10/79, 3/80, 6/80, 9/81, 2/82, 3/82, 8/82, 10/82, 2/83, 1/86
C. Denis Pegge: 4/84, 12/84
James Randi: 5/81
Tol E. Rant: 10/79
David F. Reitmeyer: 4/87
A. Grim Richardson: 5/79
Lee Russell: 1/78
Barbara S. Ryden: 4/81
James Sallis: 11/84
E. M. Schorb: 6/85
John D. Seats: 2/82, 3/82, 4/82, 7/82
Marion H. Smith: 12/80
John Stallings: 8/80
St. Maric: 8/83
Mary W. Stanton: 2/79
Peggy Tegen: 7/81
Steve Rasnic Tem: 6/81, 5/82, 7/82, 12/82, 8/83, 6/84, 8/84, 10/84, 4/85, 5/85, 7/86
Cam Thornley: 7/80
T'Pat: 9/78
William Tuning: 1/82
Steven Utley: Fall 77
A. E. van Vogt: 1/82
Peter Viereck: 11/83
Karin C. Warren: 6/85
Chris Weber: 5/82
Charles West, Jr.: 11/79
Barry Wilkes: 8/82
Nancy Tucker Wilson: 3/82
Jane Yolen: 11/80, 2/85, 6/86, 7/87, 5/88

Magazine of Fantasy and Science Fiction

Almost from its beginning in 1949, this magazine has been buying poetry in all the genres. It is hard to define a typical F&SF poem because styles have changed from decade to decade. However, ballads in the heroic mold, both serious and spoof, seem to appear frequently in its pages.

Vance Aandahl: 12/76

Karen Anderson: 5/58, 6/58, 7/62, 3/63, 5/63, 9/64, 2/65, 4/71

Poul Anderson: 10/58

Isaac Asimov: 10/54, 10/66

Mary Austin: 9/59

Ethan Ayer: 8/64

E. D. B.: 2/53

Norman Belkins: 5/59

Michael Bishop: 7/84

Ray Bradbury: 6/73, 10/76

Reginald Bretnor: 1/64

Jean Bridge: 3/64

Anthony Brode: 3/56, 5/56, 9/57, 2/58, 4/58, 2/59, 11/59, 1/60

Fredric Brown: 5/55

Edward Bryant: 3/79

Doris Pitkin Buck: 11/56, 5/57, 1/58, 2/58, 3/59, 7/59, 4/61, 7/61, 3/62, 4/62, 4/63, 5/63, 7/63, 12/64, 3/66, 4/66, 2/69, 7/70, 12/70, 6/73, 10/81

David Bunch: 6/68

Bill Butler: 8/66

John Ciardi: 1/65

Carlyn Coffin: 6/55

Christopher Corson: 5/64

M. Corwin: 6/55

Deborah Crawford: 5/65, 6/77

Avram Davidson: 8/71

L. Sprague de Camp: 1/55, 6/65, 12/66, 10/67, 9/68, 11/69, 9/70

Pat DeGrow: 6/66

Gordon Dickson: 7/54, 10/59

Thomas M. Disch: 6/79

Sonya Dorman: 10/68, 1/71, 9/72, 10/73, 6/79, 10/79, 5/80, 2/82

Leah Bodine Drake: 4/54, 7/54, 10/55, 4/57, 12/57, 8/60, 8/61, 7/64

George Alec Effinger: 8/85

Robert Frazier: 11/83, 11/86, 2/88

Randall Garrett: 10/53, 12/55, 1/60, 2/60, 5/60, 1/63

Dorothy Gilbert: 12/68

Bertrand Gironel: 3/76

Russell M. Griffin: 7/80, 2/81, 6/82

R.J.P. Hewison: 12/54

P. M. Hubbard: 5/55, 4/56, 11/58

Norman R. Jaffray: 1/54, 4/54, 2/59

Gerald Jonas: 10/79

Anne D. Jordan: 12/84

Walter H. Kerr: 2/62, 3/62, 5/62, 11/62, 6/63, 9/63, 11/64, 12/64, 3/65, 2/68, 3/73

Rudyard Kipling: 3/66

Cyril Kornbluth: 7/57

R. A. Lafferty: 3/84

Fritz Leiber: 7/69

C. Day Lewis: 2/57

C. S. Lewis: 6/59, 7/64

Henry M. Littlefield: 1/72

Archibald MacLeish: 10/63

Barry Malzberg: 2/70

Richard Matheson: 2/63
Winona McClintic: 6/53, 7/53,
    8/53, 12/53, 12/54, 3/55,
    4/55, 1/56, 6/56, 7/56, 11/57,
    3/58, 9/59
Herman W. Mudgett: 8/51, 8/53,
    9/54, 1/55, 7/55
Ogden Nash: 7/55
Jim Neal: 10/81
Starr Nelson: 10/56, 11/58
Jeannette Nichols: 10/63
Nina Pettis: 9/59
John R. Pierce: 10/59
Lawrence Raab: 5/70, 2/71

Tom Rapp: 9/76
Hilbert Schenck, Jr.: 8/59, 9/59,
    4/60, 5/60, 6/60, 10/79
Bruce Simonds: 6/64
James Spencer: 1/62
Sherwood Springer: 1/54, 7/54,
    3/77, 5/77, 11/77, 6/78
John Updike: 11/61
William Jon Watkins: 1/79
Leonard Wolf: 8/52, 11/52,
    11/53, 1/54, 7/54, 10/54,
    3/57
Jane Yolen: 6/82, 10/87

Magazine of Horror

This publication, along with *Startling Mystery Stories,* was founded by an old-time science fiction fan and writer, Robert Lowdnes, in 1965 and persisted for five years. Lowdnes published new horror stories by obscure writers such as Stephen King and reprinted classic horror stories by the old masters that had appeared mostly in the pages of *Weird Tales.* The two magazines reprinted a fair amount of poetry from *Weird Tales* and other publications.

R. H. D. Barham: 4/65
Robert Chambers: 4/65

Robert E. Howard: 11/65,
    Winter 65–66, Summer 67,
    1/68, 7/69, 12/69, Fall 70

New Worlds

For background information on *New Worlds* see the Introduction to this volume.

Bill Butler: 3/66, 12/68
Michael Butterworth: 11/67
Barry Cole: 9/67
Thomas M. Disch: 11/66, 11/69,
    1/70
Mike Evans: 10/68
Paul Green: 2/70, 4/70
Anthony Hayden-Guest: 4/69

Libby Houston: 5/69
Langdon Jones: 10/69
R. Glyn Jones: 1/70
Christopher Logue: 7/68
David Lunde: 3/68
George MacBeth: 7/67, 4/69,
    10/69
Peter Redgrove: 1/66

James Sallis: 2/70 D. M. Thomas: 3/68, 7/68, 2/69, 8/69, 2/70, 4/70

New Worlds Quarterly

An attempt was made to keep *New Worlds* alive as a quarterly paperback magazine during the early 1970s. Like most paperback magazine projects that were started during this period, it had a short life span.

Robert Calvert: #5, #10
Thomas M. Disch: #5
Libby Houston: #8
Mac King: #7

Philip Lopate: #5
Alfonso Tafoya: #7
D. M. Thomas: #6
William Jon Watkins: #10

Nightcry

Nightcry was a companion magazine to *Twilight Zone* from 1985 to 1987. Its editor, Allan Rodgers, bought prose and poetry that focused on psychological and surreal horror rather than supernatural horror. Unfortunately the public was not ready for any newsstand magazine devoted to horror.

Bruce Boston; Fall 86, Spring 87
Thomas Disch: Summer 87, Fall 87
Robert Frazier: Summer 86, Winter 86
John Gawsworth: Spring 87
V. K. Gibson: Spring 86
Rochelle Lynn Holt: Summer 86

David C. Kopaska-Merkel: Summer 87
A. R. Morlan: Spring 87
Lucius Shepard: Spring 87
Susan Sheppard: Winter 85, Winter 86
Ronald Terry: Spring 86

Quark

Quark was an attempt in the early 1970s to publish a paperback magazine in the *New Worlds'* mode in this country. Like most paperback magazine projects, it did not survive long.

Mario Cacchioni: #4
Sonya Dorman: #3
Marilyn Hacker: #2, #4

James Sallis: #2
George Stanley: #3

Startling Mystery Stories

This was a companion periodical to *Magazine of Horror*, published in the late 1960s.

L. Sprague de Camp: Summer 68, Spring 69
Robert E. Howard: Fall 67

Robert A. W. Lowdnes: Fall 66, Summer 67, Winter 68, Winter 69

Weird Tales

The original *Weird Tales* was published continuously from 1923 to 1954. There have been several attempts to revive *Weird Tales* since the early 1970s. In each case the magazine featured both original and reprint poetry by major horror writers. Its latest incarnation is currently under the editorship of George Scithers. So far, the poetry he has bought reflects his taste from *Isaac Asimov*, being light, humorous, and filled with references that only an erudite horror fan can fully appreciate.

Ruth Berman: Spring 88
Ray Bradbury: Summer 83
Joseph Payne Brennan: Spring 88
Stanton A. Coblentz: Fall 73
Virgil Finlay: Winter 73
Robert E. Howard: #1 (81), #2 (81), Summer 83
Frank Belknap Long: Fall 73, Summer 74
H. P. Lovecraft: Summer 73, Winter 73, Summer 74

Robert A. W. Lowdnes: #1 (81), #2 (81), #3 (Fall 74)
F. Gwynplaine MacIntyre: Spring 88
A. Merritt: Summer 73, Fall 73, Summer 74
Dorothy Quick: Summer 74
Clark Ashton Smith: #3 (Fall 81), Summer 83
Nancy Springer: Spring 88
Olaf Stapleton: Winter 73

Witchcraft & Sorcery

A short-lived, beautifully designed magazine of the early 1970s, this proved once more that glossy-sized horror magazines were not the formula for commercial success. Its poems, both original and reprint, focused more on magic rather than horror.

Lin Carter: 1/71
L. Sprague de Camp: Winter 73

Robert E. Howard: 1/71, 5/71, 10/71
Donald Sidney-Fryer: 5/71

Additional Publications

The following is a list of writers who have appeared in science fiction, horror, and fantasy magazines other than the ones noted in this section. It also includes poets who have published in *Amazing* and *Fantastic* before the Mavor period.

Andy Anderson
Startling Stories 8/52
Evan H. Appelman
Startling Stories 6/51
Isaac Asimov
Future Science Fiction #33
Science Fiction Quarterly
5/57, 1/58
Science Fiction Stories 3/56
William N. Beard
Science Ficiton Quarterly 5/56
Nelson Bond
Fantastic Universe 1/58
Frances Bove
Science Ficiton Storeis 9/56
Ray Bradbury
Galaxy 10/65
Gamma Spring 63
Miles J. Breuer
Amazing 8/67
M. Ludington Cain
Fantastic Novels Magazine
5/51, 6/51
Gregg Calkins
Infinity Science Fiction 6/58
Lee Chaytor
Fantastic Universe 10/57
Stanton Coblentz
Fantastic Novels Magazine
1/51
Edwin Corley
Thrilling Wonder Stories
2/53
L. Sprague de Camp
Science Fiction Stories 3/57

Famous Science Fiction
Spring 68
Worlds of If 3/67
Caroline Dechert
Unearth Fall 77
Miriam Allen de Ford
Worlds of Tomorrow 4/64
Philip Jose Farmer
Startling Stories 2/53
Barrie Fletcher
Startling Stories 8/52
Robert Frazier
Galaxy 7/80
Randall Garrett
Future Science Fiction #29
Science Fiction Stories 1/56,
3/56, 5/56, 9/56
Science Fiction Quarterly 2/56
Richard Butler Glaenzher
Famous Fantastic Mysteries
10/51
Allen Glasser
Fantastic 6/56
Other Worlds Science Fiction
September–October 57
Wonder Story Annual 1953
Louis M. Hobbs
Famous Fantastic Mysteries
6/52, 2/53, 6/53
John Jakes
Fantasy Book #7
Dorothy Jones
World of If 9/68
Zelda Kessler
Fantastic Universe 12/57

A. Kulik
Fantastic Story Magazine
7/53, Fall 54, Spring 55
Startling Stories 8/53, 10/53,
Spring 54, Summer 54, Fall
54
Thrilling Wonder Stories
11/53, Winter 54
SF Yearbook #1 (1967)
Alan Lindsey
Science Fantasy #43
Lillith Lorraine
Super Science Stories 6/51
Robert Lowdnes
Science Fiction Quarterly 8/56
John L. Magnus, Jr.
Thrilling Wonder Stories 2/53
Ib Melchior
Gamma Fall 63
James D. O'Dell
Spaceway 10/69
Alexander Samalman
Fantastic Story Magazine
Winter 55

Startling Stories Fall 55
Thrilling Wonder Stories 8/53
Irene Sekula
Fantastic Story Magazine
Spring 54, Summer 54
Robert Silverberg
Science Fiction Stories 9/56
John Squire
Worlds of If 3/61
Alfred I. Tooke
Fantastic Story Magazine
9/53
Ralph K. Wade
Startling Stories 1/53
John Walston
Fantastic Story Magazine
9/53
Richard Wilson
Science Fiction Quarterly 5/56
Michael Wolf
Fantasy Book #8
J. B. Wood
Startling Stories 10/52
SF Yearbook #1 (1967)

Small-Press Genre Magazines

These eleven small-press magazines are important showcases for science fiction, fantasy, and horror poetry. I am defining as "small press" any magazine that does not have regular newsstand distribution and pays for all its material, though at subcommercial rates. As with other literary forms, the small-press magazine has played an important role in the development of genre poetry, a role mentioned earlier in the introductory historical review.

The magazines listed below have diverse goals and outlooks. However, they have three common characteristics. They are currently being published, they have appeared at least four times, and, with the exception of *Dreams and Nightmares* for a short period in its history, they have always been paid for poetry.

Under each magazine is a list of poets published with issue information. Issues are indicated by number rather than date of appearance. When two numbers are listed separated by a slash, they refer to volume and issue number. When numbers are separated by an ampersand, that indicates a double issue.

Beyond

Fanzines are amateur publications devoted to discussing all aspects of science fiction and science fiction fan activities. They are important vehicles of fandom. Very few fanzine editors have become involved in publishing small-press magazines. *Beyond*, begun in 1985, is one of the few small-press magazines founded by fanzine editors. The editors, Shirley Winston and Roberta Rogow, have been particularly active members of Star*Trek fandom, a most vociferous group of science fiction fans who generate hundreds of fanzines. *Beyond,* which focuses on science fiction adventure, has the rather casual look associated with a typical fanzine.

Benedict Auer: #8
J. M. Benson: #7
Ruth Berman: #4, #8
William Borden: #1, #4
Edward Cohen: #5
Dan Crawford: #3, #8
Vonnie Crist: #2
Jo Anna Dale: #7, #10, #11
Keith Daniels: #7
Denise Dumars: #1
Gerald England: #3
Aisha Eshe: #2
Harold Feld: #7
Fred Finale: #3
Gregory FitzGerald: #10
Scott E. Green: #3, #4
Morgan Griffith: #3
James Lee: #6
Edward Lodi: #2
Dewi McS (pseud. for David M. Skov): #5, #6, #9

Linda Mercedes: #11
Kim L. Neidigh: #7
Steven C. Norwood: #10
Ron Offen: #10
Claire Puneky: #8
Tom Rentz: #5
Mark Rich: #4, #5
Louise Rogow: #2
Roberta Rogow: #2
Marcus Rosenblum: #11
Brett Rutherford: #10
Teresa Sarick: #1
Andrea Schlect: #8
Richard Paul Schmonsees: #10
Margaret Baliff Simon: #7
Duane Smolke: #8
Genevieve Stephens: #11
D. M. Vosk (pseud. for David M. Skov): #2, #3, #4, #7, #8
Roland A. Wakefield: #3
t. winter-Damon: #3, #4

Dreams and Nightmares

This magazine is one of only three small-press genre magazines that specialize in poetry. Its focus, as its title implies, has always been surreal fantasy, such as thoughts that may occur to a sleeping person. In the middle of its publication history, *Dreams and Nightmares* briefly became a non-paying market, a situation that lasted for only a short period because its editors stopped getting quality material. The magazine was started in 1986.

Rane Arroyo: #12, #13
Hillary Bartholomew: #7
Bruce Boston: #11, #15, #18, #19 & 20
Brian Clark: #4
Anthony Cooney: #15, #17

Gary William Crawford: #18
Vonnie Crist: #7
Keith Allen Daniels: #12 & 13, #14, #18
Geri Davis: #7
Denise Dumars: #5

Stanley A. Fellman: #18, #19 & 20

Jim Flosdorf: #19 & 20

Janet Fox: #5, #19 & 20, #22

Robert Frazier: #10, #14, #18

Chris Friend: #11

Joey Froehlich: #23

Chasen Gaver: #7

Scott E. Green: #6

John Grey: #15, #16, #17, #18, #19 & 20, #23

Genine Hahns: #19 & 20, #23

Lawrence Harding: #2, #3, #6, #14, #18, #21, #22

Dwight E. Humphries: #12 & 13

ave jeanne: #4, #6

Arthur R. Joyce: #21

Millea Kenin: #7

David C. Kopaska-Merkel: #1, #3, #4, #9, #10, #12 & 13, #14, #19 & 20

Richard Kownacki: #19 & 20

Lisa Kucharski: #14, #16, #17, #21

Mira Teru Kurka: #23

Lisa Lepovetsky: #6, #8, #9, #10, #19 & 20

Patrick McKinnon: #5

Kat Meade: #19 & 20

Robert Randolph Medcalf, Jr.: #23

Krzystof Ostaszewski: #7, #8, #19 & 20

Michael Paul Peter: #23

Beverly Poston: #22

Stan Proper: #19 & 20, #21, #22

Wendy Rathbone: #22

J. P. Reedman: #10, #11, #16, #23

Wayne Allen Sallee: #3, #4, #5, #6, #7, #8, #9, #11, #14, #15, #19 & 20, #23

Robert J. Savino: #22

Ann K. Schwader: #18

Glen Sheldon: #11, #12 & 13

M. B. Simon: #17

Mark Slatcher: #14

Gloundan Smorpian: #12 & 13

Steve Sneyd: #22, #23

Alan Stewart: #12 & 13

W. Gregory Stewart: #12 & 13, #19 & 20

James Tate: #16

Scott C. Virtes: #9, #10, #15, #19 & 20

Bobby G. Warner: #11, #14

t. Winter-Damon: #5, #11

Ree Young: #12 & 13, #15, #17

Haunts

Founded in 1984, *Haunts* is one of a large group of small-press magazines that specializes in horror. The magazine is a showcase for modern horror, both in prose and poetry. The style of horror is generally ultraviolent and frequently has no supernatural themes in the plot. If there is a supernatural component, it is frequently obscurely described.

Dan Carl Clare: #6

George Diezel II: #3

Scott E. Green: Winter 87

R. G. Hernandez: #6

Geoffrey A. Landis: Spring 88

Trace T. Maknis: Spring 88

Christine Malenfant: #6

Naima: #2

Thomas A. Rentz: #5
Richard Rosell: #6
John B. Rosenman: Spring 88
Patricia Russo: #1

Brett Rutherford: Spring 87, Fall 87
Wayne Allen Sallee: Spring 87
Richard Toelly: #4

Magazine of Speculative Poetry

Started in 1984, this magazine focuses primarily on poetry about science and scientists rather than science fiction poetry. As with any publication, the definitions may not be precisely delineated. Frequently it is a showcase for poets not particularly associated with any of the genres.

Duane Ackerson: 1/1, 1/2
Peggy Sue Alberhasky: 1/3
Brian Aldiss: 2/1, 2/2
R. Bartkowech: 1/1
Alberto Blanco: 1/2
Harry Bose: 1/3
Bruce Boston: 1/1, 1/3, 2/1, 2/2
Melissa Cannon: 1/1
Ellin E. Çarter: 1/2
G. O. Clark: 2/2
Valerie Nieman Colander: 2/2
Michael R. Collins: 2/2
S. R. Compton: 1/1, 1/3, 1/4, 2/2
Roger Dutcher: 2/1
Ron Ellis: 2/1
Michael Finley: 1/1, 1/2, 1/3
Janet Fox: 1/1
Robert Frazier: 1/1, 1/2, 1/3, 1/4, 2/1, 2/2
Philip Fried: 1/4
Robert Fromberg: 1/4
Terry A. Garey: 1/2, 2/2

Margaret Gordon-Espe: 2/2
Andrew Joron: 1/1, 2/2
Melinda Levokove: 1/1
John Wingo Long: 2/1, 2/2
Elissa Malcohn: 1/3, 1/4, 2/2
Robert Randolph Medcalf, Jr.: 1/3
A. McA. Miller: 1/2
Bonnie Morris: 1/3
Sheila E. Murphy: 2/2
Ron Nance: 1/1, 1/4
Krzysztof M. Ostazewski: 1/2, 1/3
Isabelle Perrin: 2/2
Ken Poyner: 2/2
Stan Proper: 1/3, 1/4
Mark Rich: 1/2, 1/3, 2/1, 2/2
John Oliver Simon: 1/3
William Slattery: 1/2
Steve Sneyd: 2/1
William Jon Watkins: 2/2
Robert F. Whisler: 2/4

New Pathways

For inexplicable reasons, small-press publications that focus on fantasy or horror tend to survive while hard science fiction small-press magazines frequently disappear after one or two issues. *New Pathways* is one of the small-press science fiction magazines that has survived.

The theme of its poetry is the same as that of its prose; unsentimental work with a preference for human/alien contact. The magazine started publication in 1985.

Robert Frazier: #4
Scott E. Green: #4
Patricia Jeres: #6

Rob Hollis Miller: #6
Cher Ryl: #6
Don Webb: #8

Owlflight

Owlflight has no special bent. Its editor, Millea Kenin, seems to like every form and every genre of poetry. Owlflight is one of those magazines that can truthfully claim that anyone wo has been or might have been or may become a major genre poet has appeared in its pages. From a writer's point of view, it has the unfortunate habit of appearing every one and a half to two years since its start in 1981.

V. Brigoli Armamento: #3
D. J. Baker: #5
Richard Bastian: #5
John Bell: #5
Susanne Bernhardt: #5
Donna Berns: #2
John Gregory Betancourt: #5
Morgan Brondum: #4
Marion Cohen: #4
Michael R. Collings: #2, #3, #5
S. R. Compton: #2
Robert A. Cook: #2
Marilyn Crane: #1, #2
Cathy Young Czapla: #5
Keith Allen Daniels: #2, #5
Steve Eng: #5
Patricia Fillingham: #5
Frank Finale: #5
Don Fioto: #2, #3
Janet Fox: #5
Robert Frazier: #2, #3
Joey Froehlich: #1, #4
Scott E. Green: #1, #2, #3, #4, #5
Morgan Griffith: #1, #2
John A. Haliburton: #3

R. S. Harding: #5
Elizabeth Harrod: #2
Susan Henderson: #5
R. David Holdaway: #2
Thelma Ireland: #4
K. L. Jones: #2
Penny Kemp: #5
John Kremer: #5
Frances Langelier: #5
Randall Larson: #2
Ruth Lechlitner: #4
Esther M. Leiper: #2
Ligi: #3, #4
Rebecca Lyons: #5
Robert Randolph Medcalf, Jr.: #3
Jim Neal: #5
Cady Newlin: #2
Martha Nichok: #5
Marie Redbird Parcell: #1
D. M. Rowles: #5
Jessica Amanda Salmonson: #4
Dean Allen Schreck: #4
John Oliver Simon: #3
Steve Sneyd: #5
Merle Talliaferro: #3

C. Taylor: #5
Gail Todd: #1
Kendra Usack: #5
D. M. Vosk (pseud. of David
    Skov): #2
Leilah Wendell: #4

Thomas Wiloch: #2, #5
Billy Wolfenbarger: #2, #3
Mark Worden: #3, #5
Christine Zawadiwsky: #3
Paul Edwin Zimmer: #5

Pandora

It is remarkable that *Pandora* has survived since its first issue in 1980. It has been through three different sets of owners. Further, its editorial tastes keep changing. Originally its prose and poetry tended toward surreal plots with a feminist slant. Later, much of the poetry has been satires on the genre.

Duane Ackerson: #1
Millard Alexander: #10, #13
W. S. Allen: #10
Eleanor Arnason: #16
Cindy Bakie: #3
Lee Ballentine: #14
William R. Barrow: #8
Bruce Boston: #14
Ray Bradbury: #18
Dan Brady: #3
Jane Carpenter: #2
Ellin Carter: #17
Lucille Coleman: #7
Steve Cottage: #3
Keith Allen Daniels: #8, #17
Tom Disch: #4, #6, #9
Roger Dutcher: #15
Marguerite A. Emmons: #14
Steve Eng: #5, #6, #7
Io Vanessa Feigen: #3, #6
Robert Frazier: #11, #12, #14,
    #15, #16, #17
Chris Gilbert: #12, #13
Malcolm Glass: #10
Albert Goldbarth: #14
Scott E. Green: #10, #14
William H. Green: #17

James Hamby: #13
Elissa L. A. Hamilton (pseud. for
    Elissa Malcohn): #14
June Hirsch: #1
Sharon Jackson: #1
Bill Johnson: #8
Teresa Jordan: #2
Tess Meara Kolney: #14
Geoffrey A. Landis: #17
Sandra Lindow: #17, #18
Jean Lorrah: #7
Steven Edward McDonald: #7
Lewis Lares Medina: #17
A. McA. Miller: #11
Edward Mycue: #18
Norman Nathan: #16
K. Cassandra O'Malley: #17
Alan Rice Osborne: #16
Steve Rasnic (earlier pseud. for
    Steve Rasnic Tem): #1
Wendy Rathbone: #16, #17
Tom Rentz: #18
Mark Rich: #14, #16, #17
Bruce P. Rogers: #3
D. M. Rowles: #3
Albert Russo: #4
Ann K. Schwader: #17

Daryl Scroggins: #11
Elizabeth Thomas: #18
Brun Thompson: #11
Rainbow T'Pyr: #4, #5, #7, #8, #14

M. A. Turzillo: #17
D. M. Vosk (pseud. of David Skov): #15
William M. White: #12
Lois Wickstrom: #4, #11

Scavenger's Newsletter

Started in 1981, *Scavenger's Newsletter* is a market newsletter for artists and writers that also publishes poetry. Its editor, Jane Fox, is well known for her horror stories in which bad things happen to bad people and worse things happen to good people. Her taste in poetry is the same.

Larry Baukin: #25
Sue C. Bever: #43
Bruce Boston: #10, #14, #15, #23, #27
G. Sutton Breiding: #36, #48
David R. Bunch: #30
Randy Chandler: #40
Lucile Coleman: #9, #12
S. R. Compton: #45
Dan Crawford: #50
Vonnie Crist: #35
Gregory Cross: #5, #37
Jo Anna Dale: #40, #43
Keith Allen Daniels: #28, #31, #37, #42, #46
Geri Eileen Davis: #38
Denise Dumars: #9, #18, #48, #50
Roger Dutcher: #29, #34, #42, #46
Stanley A. Fellman: #42
Margaret Flanagan (as Margaret Flanagan Eicher): #15, #22
Jean A. Frame: #41
Robert Frazier: #1, #2, #4, #10, #16, #22, #27, #32, #33, #37, #41, #48
Joey Froehlich: #1, #3, #10, #13, #17, #20, #25, #28, #31, #36, #39, #44, #45, #48

Mary Gilbert: #41
Scott E. Green: #30
D. A. Greenan: #7
John Grey: #35, #46
Carol E. Hall: #12
Elizabeth Hillman: #42
Eva Jones: #11, #50
Andrew Joron: #16
Troxey Kemper: #49
David C. Kopaska-Merkel: #31, #38, #39, #40
Paul Lambo: #14
Ron Leming: #16, #26
Lisa Lepovetsky: #23, #31
Jonathan Levant: #48
John Maclay: #18, #46
Elissa Malcohn: #44
Sharon E. Martin: #47
Lance Mazmanian: #32
Todd Mecklem: #47, #48
A. R. Morlan: #43
Edward Mycue: #44
Jim Neal: #25
Dan Opalenik: #21
John Phillips Palmer: #32, #35, #50
Audrey Parente: #8
Janet P. Reedman: #44

Tom Rentz: #26, #33, #45

Mark Rich: #27, #29, #45

Rebecca Alsup Riley: #49

Wayne Allen Sallee: #24, #33, #37

Richard J. Savino: #14

Robin Schone: #34

Ann K. Schwader: #49

Doris Selinski: #18

Cliff Simms: #34

M. B. Simon: #29, #36, #39, #45, #49

Chris Smith: #8, #17, #21, #26

Steve Sneyd: #7, #8, #10, #14, #18, #19, #22, #29, #35, #39, #45, #46, #49

Stephanie Stearns: #6, #21

Richard Toelly: #11

Scott C. Virtes: #50

D. M. Vosk: #12, #13, #18, #24, #31, #33, #39

Bob Warner: #13, #15, #24, #28, #34, #38

Susan Lilas Wiggs: #19, #38

t. Winter-Damon: #13, #23, #32

Billy Wolfenbarger: #5, #11, #20, #34, #39

Star*Line

The official newsletter of the Science Fiction Poetry Association, *Star*Line*, founded in 1978, is probably the only official publication of a writers group that pays for its material. In fact its payment policy was established to make sure that at least somewhere in the vast English-speaking literary world there would be a place that would use science fiction, fantasy, or horror poetry. *Star*Line* seems to be the one place where many professional science fiction writers display their skills as poets. Many poets who work in mainstream markets publish in *Star*Line*. Oddly enough, relatively few poets who started their career in genre small-press markets appear here. On the other hand, *Star*Line* has been the first science fiction poetry appearance for many writers. The annual Rhysling issues are listed separately under the entry for the Rhysling Awards Anthology Chapbook series.

Duane Ackerson: 1/4, 1/10, 1/12, 2/1, 2/2, 2/6, 6/1, 6/3, 6/4, 6/5, 8/1, 8/6, 9/2, 10/5

Brian W. Aldiss: 5/3, 6/1

Colleen Anderson: 11/2

Ivan Arguelles: 7/1, 7/2, 8/2, 10/4

Hope Athearn: 8/5, 9/2

Elspeth Aubrey: 6/5

D. A. Bach: 11/2

Lee Ballentine: 5/1, 5/3, 5/4, 5/5, 10/1

Gary Beck: 8/5

Ruth Berman: 2/1, 8/6

Frank C. Bertrand: 1/3

John Gregory Betancourt: 4/5

Sue C. Bever: 9/2, 10/3, 11/1

Anne Binch: 2/4 & 5, 7/1, 9/4

Michael Bishop: 5/4

Sandra Black: 11/1

R. A. Boris: 6/3

Harry Bose: 3/3, 4/2, 7/3

Mo Bose: 1/5, 1/6, 1/8, 1/11, 1/12, 2/3, 2/8, 2/12

Bruce Boston: 1/11, 1/12, 2/1, 2/6, 2/8, 2/10, 2/11, 3/1, 3/2, 3/3, 3/6, 4/2, 4/3, 4/5, 5/1, 5/3, 5/4, 6/1, 6/3, 6/4, 6/6, 7/1, 8/1, 8/5, 10/4, 10/5

Steve Bowkett: 9/3, 10/1

Marion Zimmer Bradley: 3/6

Gary Brown: 1/4

David R. Bunch: 4/6, 7/1, 8/4

Sandra Stuart Burkhardt: 4/5

Jack Butler: 10/3, 10/4, 10/6

Melissa Cannon: 8/1

Orson Scott Card: 3/4

Alan Catlin: 56

James Cervantes: 10/6

Betty Chancellor: 9/6

Robert M. Chute: 9/5

Marcia Cohee: 10/2

Mitchell C. Cohen: 8/6, 9/3, 9/5, 9/6

Valerie Collander: 6/5

Lucile Coleman: 6/5

Michael Collings: 4/2, 4/5, 4/6, 5/4, 5/5, 5/6, 6/5, 6/6, 9/4, 10/1, 11/2

S. R. Compton: 2/4 & 5, 2/8, 2/9, 6/1, 6/6, 9/4, 9/5

Anthony Cooney: 9/6

Wesli Court: 5/6

Gary Crawford: 8/2

Vonnie Crist: 10/1

J. L. Cuppy: 10/6

Betsy Curtis: 2/4 & 5, 2/8

K. Allen Daniels: 2/3, 2/9, 3/1, 3/2, 3/3, 3/6, 5/3, 5/4, 9/1, 9/3, 9/4, 9/5, 9/6, 10/5, 11/1, 11/2

Jack Dann: 7/1

Harry Davidov: 5/3, 6/3

Avram Davidson: 6/5

Stephen W. Dickinson: 2/4 & 5

Tom Digby: 7/3

Peter Dillingham: 1/2, 1/5, 1/11

Tom Disch: 4/3, 8/4

C. Clark Donaldson, Jr.: 7/3

James S. Dorr: 10/3

Alix Dove: 2/10

Jacques DuLumiere: 6/4

Denise Dumars: 8/6, 9/5, 10/5

Patricia Dunn: 8/6

Roger Dutcher: 6/2, 9/6

Thomas A. Easton: 10/6, 11/2

Helen Ehrlich: 7/1, 8/1, 8/4, 9/2, 9/3, 10/4, 10/6

Suzette H. Elgin: 1/2, 1/5, 1/6, 1/8, 1/9, 1/10, 1/12, 2/3, 2/4 & 5, 2/10, 2/11, 2/12, 3/1, 3/2, 3/3, 5/2, 5/3, 5/4, 6/2, 10/5

Ron Ellis: 7/1, 8/2, 11/2

Steve Eng: 4/3, 7/1

B. Buckley Finnegan: 8/3, 8/6, 9/1

James Fowler: 9/4

Janet Fox: 3/3, 3/4, 4/2, 4/5, 5/4, 8/2

Robert Frazier: 1/5, 1/8, 1/10, 1/11, 2/1, 2/6, 3/2, 5/5, 7/2

Mary Fredericks: 1/11

Tim Friel: 3/3, 3/4

Camp Gaar: 10/4, 10/6

Terry Garey: 4/6, 5/4, 7/1, 10/6

Gail Ghai: 8/6

Loss Glazier: 8/3

Felix C. Gottschalk: 4/5

Scott E. Green: 2/8, 2/9, 3/2, 3/4, 5/3

John Francis Haines: 6/4

Joe Haldeman: 6/6

John A. Haliburton: 1/4

Elissa L. A. Hamilton (pseud. for Elissa Malcohn): 4/2, 4/3,

4/5, 4/6, 5/3, 5/5
Fritz Hamilton: 5/1
Terry Hansen: 2/2
Carl S. Harker: 7/3
Marshall Harvey: 9/6, 10/4
Miriam Hasert: 5/1, 6/2
Donald M. Hassler: 11/2
Becky Hayworth: 6/2
Janie Helser: 6/1
Tom Henighan: 11/1
Ken Hill: 8/5
Rochelle Lynn Holt: 9/5
Akua Lezli Hope: 9/4
Judith Horan: 9/3
Lyle Howard: 6/2
John Huotari: 8/5
Charles Carter Jacob: 9/1
Dale Jensen: 7/2
George Clayton Johnson: 3/3
Karen Jollie: 2/3, 2/4 & 5, 2/6,
    2/8, 2/10, 2/11, 2/12, 3/6,
    4/2, 5/3
Andrew Joron: 1/12, 4/2, 4/5, 6/1,
    8/1, 8/2
Emil Kay: 2/12, 3/1, 3/6
Scott A. Kelly: 10/4
Jean McClure Kelty: 5/4, 6/2
Millea Kenin: 4/2, 8/4
Michael Ketchek: 10/6
Annette Curtis Klause: 4/6, 6/5,
    9/1
David C. Kopaska-Merkel: 9/4,
    9/5, 9/6, 10/3, 10/6, 11/1
Frances Langelier: 7/2, 8/5, 9/1,
    10/2, 10/3, 10/4
Ursula K. LeGuin: 5/1, 8/2, 8/6
Esther Leiper: 4/5
James Lipscomb: 3/2
David Lunde: 4/6, 5/1, 5/3, 5/4,
    6/1, 6/2, 8/6
Jack Lundy: 10/6, 11/1
Alan Lupack: 9/6

Ron Maggiano: 8/6, 9/4
Elissa Malcohn: 6/2, 6/4, 6/6,
    7/2, 8/5
Hank Mannheimer: 10/4
Elizabeth Marion: 10/2
Sue Marra: 6/6
Michael Marsh: 5/6, 6/2
Sally Marshall: 8/3
Pat Martinelli: 9/2, 9/4
Cyn Mason: 6/1
Clive Matson: 8/3
Carol V. Matuszak: 3/2, 3/4
Frederick J. Mayer: 1/2, 4/1
Steven Edward McDonald: 2/4 &
    5, 3/1, 3/2, 3/4, 4/1, 4/3
Donald McLeod: 11/2
Robert Medcalf, Jr.: 4/2, 4/5, 5/5,
    6/2
Lewis Medina: 9/2
Terry Mollohan: 8/6
Mario Montalbetti: 6/4
Edward Mycue: 7/3
B. Z. Niditch: 8/2, 9/5
Clay Norris: 1/10, 2/3
Susan Packie: 6/6
Bob Paquin: 6/4
Peter Payack: 3/4, 4/2
Kevin Pehr: 7/2
Georgette Perry, 5/1, 9/2
Terry L. Persun: 5/3
David Piercy: 7/1
Marge Piercy: 6/4
Rachel Pollack: 6/1
Jonathan V. Post: 6/6, 9/6
Ken Poyner: 10/4, 10/6
David Prill: 6/6
Stan Proper: 10/3
Kathryn Rantala: 1/12, 4/1, 4/2,
    4/3, 5/3, 5/5, 6/1, 6/4, 8/4
Wendy Rathbone: 8/5, 8/6, 9/1,
    9/3, 10/1, 10/5
Bonnie Rauscher: 2/4 & 5

Melanie A. Rawls: 9/5, 10/6, 11/2

Jonathan Raz: 2/1, 4/2, 4/5, 5/6, 6/1, 6/2, 8/6

Tom Rentz: 9/6

Mark Rich: 7/1, 8/4, 9/2, 9/5, 10/1, 10/2

Tom Riley: 9/1, 9/2, 9/5, 9/6, 10/1, 10/2, 10/3, 10/4, 10/5, 10/6, 11/1

Greg Robel: 10/3

M. M. Roessner-Herman: 4/5

Wendy Rose: 5/1, 5/3

Dorothy M. Ross: 5/4

Chuck Rothman: 10/3, 11/1

Susan Noe Rothman: 9/2, 9/3, 9/4, 9/5, 10/3, 10/4

Albert Russo: 5/1

Miriam Sagan: 5/5, 5/6

Wayne Allen Sallee: 10/1

Jessica Amanda Salmonson: 6/3, 8/1, 8/2

Lorraine Schein: 4/1, 6/2, 9/2

Andrea Schlecht: 10/3

Dean Allen Schreck: 6/6

Roger Schroeder: 9/2

Lyn Schumaker: 5/5

Ann K. Schwader: 10/1, 10/6, 11/1, 11/2

Marilyn Shea: 10/6

Lucius Shepard: 10/5

John Shirley: 4/1

John Oliver Simon: 4/2

Marge Ballif Simon: 9/4, 10/1

Haydn Sloan: 8/3

Julie A. Smith: 6/2, 6/6

Loretta M. Smith: 6/1, 6/2

Steve Sneyd: 1/11, 2/1, 2/3, 2/12, 3/1, 3/4, 4/2, 4/5, 4/6, 5/5, 6/1, 6/4, 6/6, 7/1, 9/3, 9/4, 9/6, 10/2

Margaret Somers: 8/3

Rhea Sossen: 7/1

Douglas Spangle: 7/2, 7/3, 8/3, 8/4

Nancy Springer: 4/5, 5/6

William Stafford: 6/4, 6/5

Craig Peter Standish: 7/3

H. Starr: 5/1

Richard Stevenson: 9/2

Alan Stewart: 9/2, 10/3, 11/2

J. T. Stewart: 6/4

W. Gregory Stewart: 9/3, 9/5, 9/6, 10/1, 10/2, 10/3, 10/4, 11/1, 11/2

Michael Stiles: 9/6, 10/2, 10/3

Susanna J. Sturgis: 10/1

Jorge Tellier: 6/4

Steve Rasnic Tem: 7/2

Judy Tote: 6/3

Linda Tremblay: 9/4

Lewis Turco: 5/6

Frederick Turner: 4/6

Steven M. Tymon: 2/4 & 5, 4/1

Jim Van Pelt: 10/1

Gene Van Troyer: 2/8, 3/2, 4/3

Marcia Van Wyck: 8/5, 9/2, 9/3

Ralph E. Vaughan: 4/5

William J. Vernon: 5/1, 5/3

Joan D. Vinge: 4/2

D. M. Vosk (pseud. of David Skov): 11/1

Terri H. Smith Wallace: 5/6

Don Webb: 10/3

James P. Werbaneth: 10/1

Charles West: 8/4

Neal Wilgus: 1/11, 2/1, 2/3, 4/2, 5/5, 6/5, 7/1, 8/5, 9/1, 10/1

Carl Mike Williams: 6/3, 6/4

Paul O. Williams: 1/8, 1/11, 2/10

Thomas Wiloch: 5/4, 6/2, 6/3, 10/1

t. Winter-Damon: 9/2

Gene Wolfe: 3/3, 4/2, 4/3, 5/3

Billy Wolfenbarger: 9/5

Peter Wyman: 6/5

Bart Yoder: 1/8

Jane Yolen: 4/3, 4/5, 5/1, 5/3, 5/6, 8/1, 8/2, 8/3

Ree Young: 10/5, 11/2

Roger Zelazny: 5/3

Paul Edwin Zimmer: 7/1, 8/5

2 A.M.

2 A.M., founded in 1986, is another contemporary horror small-press magazine that has become an important showcase for poetry.

Leonard Carpenter: 1/3

Darwin Chismar: 1/2

H. J. Cording: 1/2

Arthur Winfield Knight: 2/1

Lisa Lepovetsky: 1/1, 1/3

Sue Marra: 1/3

Sheryl Nelms: 2/1

Jay Owen: 1/1

Marthayn Pelegrimas: 1/2, 1/3

Margie Penn-Freeman: 2/1

Mark Rich: 1/4

William P. Robertson: 1/1

Doris Selinski: 2/1

Lee Ann Sontheimer: 2/1

Roger Dale Trexler: 1/4

D. M. Vosk (pseud. of David Skov): 1/1

Z Miscellaneous

Z Miscellaneous is a mainstream literary magazine that has been an important showcase for genre poets since 1986. This role was formerly undertaken by Pulpsmith before it became an annual. Even the work done by nongenre poets is frequently surreal and light fantasy. This does not mean that most mainstream poets are closet science fiction or fantasy writers. Rather, it indicates that what can be considered genre themes form an important part of poetry in general. A poet is described by the venue of his or her work as much as by the theme or purpose of the work.

Katharyn Machan Aal: 1/3

Loretta Adrian: 1/2

Peggy Sue Alberhasky: 1/1

Rane Arroyo: 1/3

Lili Artel: 1/4

Benedict Auer: 1/3

Jim Auer: 1/1

Dick Bakken: 1/2, 1/3

Elizabeth Bartlett: 1/4

Conger Beasley, Jr.: 1/3, 1/4

Jack B. Bedell: 1/4

Rodney D. Bell: 1/3

Richard G. Beyer: 1/3, 1/4

Bruce Boston: 1/1, 1/4

Jennifer Welch Bosveld: 1/3

Joseph Bruchac: 1/4

Gray Burr: 1/3

Brett Campbell: 1/3

Crystal Carmen: 1/3, 1/4
Ann Carter: 1/4
Luanne Castle: 1/4
D. Castleman: 1/3
Alan Catlin: 1/3
Joyce A. Chandler: 1/1, 1/4
Michael Chandler: 1/3
Michele J. Charvet: 1/3
David Chorlton: 1/1, 1/2, 1/4
G. O. Clark: 1/3
Wanda Coleman: 1/3
Jean Colonomos: 1/3
Robert Cooperman: 1/3, 1/4
Steven R. Cope: 1/4
Cathy Czapla: 1/4
Charles Darling: 1/3
Tony D'Arpino: 1/3
Jon Daunt: 1/2
Susan Stranger Deal: 1/4
Lorraine S. Degennaro: 1/1
Sue DeKelver: 1/3
S. H. Dewhurst: 1/2
Paul Dilsaver: 1/4
Jill Dimaggio: 1/1
John Ditsky: 1/3
Bella Donna: 1/2, 1/4
Julian Nunnally Duncan: 1/3
Ann Dunn: 1/4
W. D. Ehrhart: 1/3
Margaret Flanagan Eicher: 1/4
Sue Saniel Elkind: 1/1, 1/3, 1/4
Richard Elman: 1/4
Gerald England: 1/3
Aisha Eshe: 1/1, 1/2, 1/4
Hannah Margaret Estabrooks:
    1/1, 1/4
Richard Fein: 1/3, 1/4
Al Feldman: 1/3
H. R. Felgenhauer: 1/3
Katherine Flanagan-Simpson:
    1/2
Kurt Flickert: 1/4

David Flynn: 1/3
Janet Fox: 1/1
Walt Franklin: 1/2, 1/3
David K. Fujino: 1/3
Norman German: 1/2
Diane Glancy: 1/4
Emilie Glen: 1/3
George Golt: 1/4
Eugene V. Grace: 1/1, 1/2
Benjamin Green: 1/1
Kelly Green: 1/3
John Grey: 1/1, 1/2, 1/4
Andrew J. Grossman: 1/2
M. B. Hamilton: 1/4
Jean Harmon: 1/2, 1/4
Joseph Harris: 1/4
Gayle Elen Harvey: 1/1, 1/4
Patricia Harwin: 1/3
Peggy Heinrich: 1/4
Mary Ann Henn: 1/4
Bernard Hewitt: 1/3
Wayne Hogan: 1/3
John J. Holden: 1/4
Rochelle Lynn Holt: 1/2
Carolyn J. Fairweather Hughes:
    1/3
Sophie Hughes: 1/3
John Hurley: 1/4
Will Inman: 1/1, 1/2, 1/4
Gray Jacobik: 1/3
Jiri Jirasek: 1/3
Robert K. Johnson: 1/1, 1/3
Allan Johnston: 1/4
Susan Katz: 1/2, 1/3
Philip Keinholz: 1/3
Ruth Moon Kempher: 1/1
Joan Payne Kincaid: 1/3
Ronald Edward Kittell: 1/3
Arthur Winfield Knight: 1/1,
    1/3
William James Kovanda: 1/3,
    1/4

Janet Krauss: 1/3
Mindy H. Kronenberg: 1/4
Elsie Bowman Kurz: 1/2
Jonathan Levant: 1/1, 1/3
Danny Lewis: 1/4
Lyn Lifshin: 1/3, 1/4
Janet Lombard: 1/3
Celia S. Lustgarten: 1/3
Janice M. Lynch: 1/3
Lillian Maccabee: 1/4
Steven Malkus: 1/2
Eileen Malone: 1/4
Joanna M. Marinelli: 1/3
Steven Markus: 1/1
Janet McCann: 1/2
Jane McCray: 1/3
Jim McCurry: 1/2
Whitman McGowan: 1/4
Linda Back McKay: 1/3, 1/4
Jack McManis: 1/3
Kat Meads: 1/3
Claire Michaels: 1/2, 1/3
Tony Moffet: 1/3
Eugenia Moore: 1/3, 1/4
Lillian Morrison: 1/4
J. B. Mulligan: 1/2
Jim Murphy: 1/2, 1/3
E'Lane Carlisle Murray: 1/4
Edward Mycue: 1/4
Minerva Neiditz: 1/4
Sheryl L. Nelms: 1/1, 1/2
Eric Nelson: 1/4
Joyce Nower: 1/1
Michael E. Nowicki: 1/3, 1/4
Bruce O'Dell: 1/3
Jane M. Orvis: 1/4
Krzysztof Ostaszewski: 1/3, 1/4
Marlena Parisheva: 1/3
Marion Ford Park: 1/4
Arlie Parker: 1/3, 1/4
Anita Patterson: 1/1, 1/2, 1/4
Cynthia S. Pederson: 1/4

Barbara J. Petoskey: 1/4
Ace G. Pilkington: 1/3
Claude Planidin: 1/4
Jonathan Potter: 1/4
Marjorie Power: 1/4
John Powers: 1/4
Constance Pultz: 1/3
Wendy Rathbone: 1/1
Robin Rauch: 1/3
Daniel Remington: 1/4
Susan Richardson: 1/3
Elliot Richman: 1/3
Marijane O. Ricketts: 1/4
Kinloch Rivers: 1/4
Rosaly Demaios Roffman: 1/2, 1/3
Rose Rosberg: 1/3
Dorothy Rose: 1/3
Shelley Rozen: 1/4
Helen Ruggieri: 1/4
Don Russ: 1/1, 1/2
Wayne Allen Sallee: 1/1, 1/3
Trinidad Sanchez: 1/4
Briseida Sancho: 1/2, 1/3
Lorraine Schein: 1/3
Susan Schreibman: 1/4
Lawrence R. Schug: 1/2, 1/3
David Schuster: 1/4
Hillel Schwartz: 1/3
Pearl Bloch Segall: 1/1, 1/2, 1/4
Joseph Semenovich: 1/1, 1/4
Jack Shadoian: 1/2
Eve Sheinutt: 1/4
Alana Sherman: 1/3
Mary Crescenzo Simons: 1/4
Rosanne Singer: 1/4
Ken Smith: 1/4
James Snydal: 1/3, 1/4
Joseph Somoza: 1/3, 1/4
Lee Ann Sontheimer: 1/4
Walter Staples: 1/2
David Starkey: 1/3, 1/4

Patricia Steele: 1/3
Paula Stefan: 1/1, 1/2
Shelby Stephenson: 1/3
Gerry Stewart: 1/3
Ken Stone: 1/2
Genevieve Thompson: 1/2, 1/4
Don Thornton: 1/3
Asher Torren: 1/2, 1/3
William J. Vernon: 1/3
Martha M. Vertreace: 1/3
Gwendolyn Vincent: 1/4
Anca Vlasopolos: 1/3
Martin Wallach: 1/4

Robert R. Ward: 1/3, 1/4
Janet Lee Warman: 1/3
Paul Weinman: 1/3
Sigmund Weiss: 1/4
Dan Wilcox: 1/3
A. D. Winans: 1/3, 1/4
Kirk Wirsig: 1/4
Adrienne Wolfert: 1/4
William Woodruff: 1/3
A. J. Wright: 1/2, 1/3
John Yamrus: 1/1, 1/4
Dale G. Yerbe: 1/3

II.
Poetry in
Genre Anthologies

Key Anthologies and Anthology Series

The following is an alphabetical annotated bibliographical list of key genre poetry collections as well as other anthologies that included poetry. For the key works, those collections that have had a strong impact upon the field of genre poetry, I have included a list of contents. These anthologies and anthology series are *Aliens and Lovers, Burning with a Vision, Elsewhere, England Swings SF, Holding Your Eight Hands, Operation Phantasy, Poly,* Pournelle Anthologies, Rhysling Anthologies (including special Rhysling issues of *Star*Line*), *Songs from Unsung Worlds, The Umbral Anthology of Science Fiction Poetry,* and Vaughan Anthologies.

Following the key anthologies is another annotated list of anthologies and collections of historical rather than critical significance to science fiction, fantasy, and horror poetry. Separate lists of additional science fiction, fantasy, and horror anthologies that included poetry are then given, with poets indicated for each. Finally is a list of single-author collections that also included poetry.

I have not covered the numerous poetry anthologies that are the result of fannish activities. They lie outside of the general purview of this book.

Aliens and Lovers

Edited by Millea Kenin. Oakland, CA: Unique Graphics, 1983

Aliens and Lovers differs from the other major science fiction poetry anthologies in three signifcant ways. First, the majority of poets in this work had established their reputations as poets in genre small-press and fannish publications. In fact the editor herself is a long-established figure in genre small-press and fannish circles. Most of the writers who had appeared in the other anthologies had entered the science fiction, fantasy, and horror fields from the mainstream, where they had already established their reputations. Second, the anthology is deeply embedded in its genre roots. The language of the poems and their motifs are traditionally associated with genre science fiction, fantasy, and horror. Finally, it is a single-theme anthology devoted to erotic relationships. The other anthologies mentioned previously were general in their themes, though all of them had many erotic poems in their pages.

D. J. Baker: "Songflower"

Lee Ballentine: "Salvager"

Ruth Berman: "White Persephone"

Susanne Bernhardt: "When We Came to Earth"

John Gregory Betancourt: "Unicornucopia," "Was It You"

Bruce Boston: "Luminaries," "The Mating of the Storm Birds," "Night Flight"

Sandra Stuart Burkhardt: "Dreams of Alien Love"

Ellin Carter: "History/ Herstory," "Reply by Time Warp"

John Clarke: "you bath your clothes in sun . . ." (untitled poem)

Michael R. Collings: "Aube," "Orchisophilia"

S. R. Compton: "Blue Movie Records a Sea Change," "Poor Little Robot"

M. Crane: "Blood Ties," "The Incubus"

Cathy Young Czapla: "Basilisk"

Lari Davidson: "Pan"

Charles DeLint: "Ariane"

C. K. DeRugeris: "Horse De Fate"

Roger L. Dutcher: "Astrology: For Susan," "Comet," "The Night Caller," "Venus"

Page Virginia Else: "Leavetaking," "so if a romantic oceanographer" (untitled poem)

KEY ANTHOLOGIES AND ANTHOLOGY SERIES / 37

Steve Eng: "Night Caress," "Vaingloria"
Teri Fontaine: "Alien Country Wine," "Purifying the Apple"
Janet Fox: "In the First Month of Becoming"
Robert Frazier: "Compass Me Round with Silence"
Juanita Garciagodoy: "Nimue," "A Rose Bouquet"
Terry A. Garey: "Beach Witch," "Titan to Saturn"
Scott E. Green: "First Love," "Skirmishes Through the Hours"
Darwin Hageman: "Celestial Bodies"
Penny Kemp: "Painting"
Christina Kiplinger: "Possessed"
Albert Lannon: "She"
James A. Lee: "At Zero Gee"
Lisa F. Lomax: "And Time Glowed By"
Jonathan Lowe: "Braille"
Rebecca Lyons: "Conjugation"
D. A. Maker: "Distant Affairs"
Wendy McElroy: "The Forest During Witching Hour," "Mermaid,"
    "To Be Continued"
J. R. McHone: "Dead Heat"
Robert Randolph Medcalf, Jr.: "The Catwoman," "Green Love,"
    "Haiku," "Icegirl," "Rainbow Girl," "Witchwoman"
Pat Merritt: "Night Flight"
Pat Monaghan: "The Witch Threatened"
Rich Murphy: "Still Life/ Fifteenth Round"
Berry Nolley: "Ginny"
Susan Heyboer O'Keefe: "Zhatha"
Alanne Oliver: "The Possessor," "Sisters Across Time"
Marie Redbird Parcell: "Land Passion"
Gene Phillips: "The First Coming"
David Piercy: "Crosscurrents," "Midnight Rendezvous,"
    "Seedmaker's Song," "When Again the Glass Fluted Bloom"
David Prill: "The Girl of My Dreams Left Her Heart with
    Monsanto"
Christine Lee Quilissi: "True Mars Confession"
R. L. Robins: "Links and Lust"
Mike Romesburg: "Crossplants"
Jessica Amanda Salmonson: "The Unsuspecting"
Hillel Schwartz: "Dorothy, All Grown Up, Returns to Oz"
D. E. Smirl: "C"
Steven Sneyd: "A Taste of Salvation"
C. W. Spinks: "Animation"

Kiel Stuart: "Green Horizon"
C. Raylor: "A Little Nukie Never Hurts Anyone"
Steve Rasnic Tem: "First Contact," "The Lovers"
Kathleen Todd: "Earth Comes"
Ralph E. Vaughan: "Alien Lover," "Smokey Love"
William J. Vernon: "On Meeting A Robot"
D. M. Vosk (pseud. for David Skov): "Androidal Charms"
Deb Warhol: "The Phantom"
Harmony Water: "Study for a Sculpture"
Diana Watson: "Sirensong I," "Spirit"
Sarah Brown Weitzman: "Conservation of Matter"
Leilah Wendell: "Escape," "To My Bride"
Hans-Peter Werner: "Sirens"
Robert F. Whisler: "Like Sinsemilla"
Neal Wilgus: "Bait"

Burning with a Vision

Edited by Robert Frazier. Philadelphia: Owlswick Press, 1984.

The element of emotion has always been the most important part of Robert Frazier's poetry. For this reason he became involved in science fiction and science poetry. From his perspective these are genres of poetry where emotion is still important to the work. That is an important common thread among the poems that he purchased for this anthology.

The purpose of *Burning with a Vision* was to be more than just a showcase for science fiction poetry. Rather, it was to showcase equally poems from both science fiction genre sources as well as speculative poems from mainstream sources. Of the 131 poems, 76 came from genre science fiction sources such as newsstand magazines (*Amazing, Isaac Asimov, F & SF*), paperback anthologies (*Berkley Showcase Vol. 5*), fanzines (*Aurora*), and small press (*Owlflight, Star*Line*). Previously, anthologies had reprinted primarily speculative poems from mainstream sources.

The implication of Frazier's choice is twofold. First, it documents the establishment of poetry as a significant form of expression in American science fiction. Second, it demonstrates that the language of genre science fiction, not just its images and themes, is a legitimate and important tool for poets.

Diane Ackerman: "Ode to an Alien," "The Other Night (Comet Kohoutek)," "Whale Songs"

Duane Ackerson: "Fatalities," "The Starman"

Brian W. Aldiss: "Bridging Hour in Weseiv," "Destruction of the Fifth Planet," "Space Burial," "Thomas Hardy Considers the Newly-Published Special Theory of Relativity"

Ruth Berman: "Computative Oak"

Michael Bishop: "For the Lady of a Physicist," "Postcards to Athena," "White Power Poem"

Harry Bose: "Seven One-Line Poems"

Bruce Boston: "Defeat at the Hands of Alien Scholars," "Human Remains," "If Gravity Were Like Weather," "Mathematician," "The FTL Addict Fixes," "The Star Drifter Grounded," "Want Ad"

Edward Bryant: "Winslow Crater"

David R. Bunch: "Of Time and Us," "On Passing by Those Icy Stones"

Dave Calder: "the planets, the people" (untitled poems), "under dream interrogation" (untitled poems)

John Ciardi: "Love Letter from Mars"

S. R. Compton: "Photomicrograph: Last Centimer of the Human Airway," "The Imagination of the Retina"

Adam Cornford: "Our Sorcerers"

Jack Dann: "Ceremony," "from Hospital Songs," "Stone Stars"

Lucille Day: "Cytogenetics Lab," "Neural Folds"

Thomas M. Disch: "A Vacation on Earth," "Can You Hear Me," "Thinktank Two?," "Cosmology & Us," "In the Picture," "On Science Fiction," "Outer Space Haiku"

Raymond DiZazzo: "On the Speed of Sight"

Sonya Dorman: "A Lullaby, a Farewell," "Corruption of Metals," "On the Marriage of Art and Science," "Vanishing Points," "Wormrunner's Curse"

Roger Dutcher: "Antaeus (The Prodigious Builders)"

Loren Eiseley: "Beware, My Successor"

Suzette Haden Elgin: "McLuhan Transposed"

Philip José Farmer: "The Pterodactyl"

Jane Fox: "INSTITUTIONS," "Quotella"

Robert Frazier: "Flash Sleep," "Loren Eiseley's Time Passages," "(Senryu)"

Terry A. Garey: "Full House," "Partial View of a Supernova"

Albert Goldbarth: "Saucer Station: Monday–Friday," "Starbirth"

Phyllis Gotlieb: "Cosmology," "Haiku and 1/2," "was/man"
Joe W. Haldeman: "Saul's Death: Two Sestinas"
Bruce Hawkins: "A Great Annelid Worm," "2021:Noon:Idaho"
Andrew Joron: "Agency," "Asleep in the Arms of Mother Night,"
    "The Hunter: 20,000 A.D.," "The Sonic Flowerfall of Primes,"
    "White Noise"
Andrew Joron and Robert Frazier: "The Aging of Clones"
Ursula K. LeGuin: "Morden Lecture, 1978," "The Song of the
    Dragon's Daughter," "The Well of Baln," "The Withinner,"
    "To Siva, the Unmaker"
Alan P. Lightman: "First Rainfall"
David Lunde: "The Monster," "The Singularity in Cygnus XI
    Viewed with Pity for HDE 226868"
Elissa Hamilton Malcohn: "Wings," "Ybba"
Adrianne Marcus: "The Physicist's Purpose," "Science/Fiction,"
    "Thermodynamics"
Harry Martinson: "Hades and Euclid"
Edwin Morgan: "In Sobieski's Shield," "Instamatic The Moon
    February 1973," "Spacepoem 3: Off Course"
Peter Payack: "Assembling the World," "Microcosmos,"
    "Motorcycle Evolution," "Spinning Yarns, Relatively
    Speaking," "The Migration of Darkness"
Georgette Perry: "Neutrinos"
Jonathan V. Post: "The Neurophysiologist"
Kathryn Rantala: "Grand Mal," "Harmoniums," "Noah at Sea,"
    "Slipping in Orbit"
Wendy Rose: "Calling the Scientists Home"
John Oliver Simon: "Headlands, 2365," "The Hanged
    Man"
Steve Sneyd: "Asteroid Lil," "Astronaut's Widow," "Bright New
    Missouri," "The Lure"
Nancy Springer: "The Wolf Girl Speaks"
Steven Rasnic Tem: "ESP," "Lighting the Colony," "Unknown
    Shores"
Steven Utley: "The Local Allosaurus"
Gene Van Troyer: "The Axeltree"
Edward Wellen: "Adaption — Year 2000"
Lois Wickstrom: "MC^2=E," "A Slice of Life"
Gene Wolfe: "The Computer Iterates the Greater Trumps"
Jane Yolen: "Caliban's Song," "Death of a Unicorn," "The Fossilot,"
    "Icarus," "Metamorphosis," "Neptune Rising"

Roger Zelazny: "Dreamscapes," "I Used to Think in Lines That
   Were Irregular to the Right"
Al Zolynas: "The New Physics"

Elsewhere

Edited by Terri Windling and Mark Alan Arnold. New York: Ace
Books, Vol. I (1981); Vol. II (1982); Vol. III (1984).

Elsewhere is a three-volume anthology of reprinted and original
fantasy, both prose and poetry. The purpose of the anthology is to
demonstrate the broad range of fantasy, though it was not intended to
be a "Best Of" approach. The only common theme is that most of the
prose and poetry is concerned with that basic element of fantasy
literature, when the magical worlds thrust into the mundane.

There is no typical source for the reprinted poetry. Publications as
diverse as *The New Yorker* and *Magazine of Fantasy and Science
Fiction* are represented, along with horror fanzines, mainstream
literary magazines, and single-author collections. However, the bulk of
the reprinted poems come from single-author collections of mainstream
poets such as Lawrence Raab and Louise Gluck. Most of the original
work comes from established genre writers like James Blaylock, Tanith
Lee, Steve Rasnic Tem, and Jane Yolen.

While the series was not intended to be the definitive collection
of fantasy poetry, it has that place until something better comes
along.

Vol. I:
W. S. Gilbert: "Oh! My Name Is John Wellington Wells"
Robert Graves: "Song of Amergin"
Ursula K. LeGuin: "The Song of the Dragon's Daughter"
Harold Monro: "Overheard on a Saltmarsh"
Alastair Reid: "A Spell for Sleeping"
Masao Takiquichi: "Pale Horse"
John Alfred Taylor: "The Succubus"
William Butler Yeats: "The Hosting of the Sidhe"
Jane Yolen: "The Merman in Love"

Vol. II:
Bellamy Bach: "A Tourist Camped on a Donegal Field"
Eskimo Chant: "In the Very Earliest Time"

Andrew Glazer: "The Trash Dragon of Shensi"
Li Ho: "Magic Strings"
Ellen Kushner: "Gwydion's Loss of Llew"
Donovan Leitch: "Lord of the Reedy River"
R. P. Lister: "Haunted"
Nicholas Moore: "The Island and the Cattle"
Brian Patten: "Small Dragon"
Anne Sexton: "The Twelve Dancing Princesses"
Henry Treece: "The Magic Wood"
Peter Viereck: "Homecoming"

Vol. III:
Leonard Cohen: "God Is Alive, Magic Is Afoot"
Susan Feldman: "Intruder"
Louise Gluck: "Gretel in Darkness"
Robert Graves: "The Six Badgers"
Ramon Guthrie: "Springsong in East Gruesome, Vermont"
John Haines: "And When the Green Man Comes"
David Ignatow: "Simultaneously"
Ian McDonald and Peter Sinfield: "In the Court of the Crimson
   King"
Robert Mezey: "Being a Giant"
Lawrence Raab: "Voices Answering Back the Vampires"
William Jay Smith: "The Toaster"
John Alfred Taylor: "Princeps Tenebarum"
Richard Wilbur: "The Undead"

England Swings SF

Edited by Judith Merrill. New York: Ace Books, 1968.

Judith Merrill, as noted previously, became a major advocate of the speculative fiction and poetry being published in the English magazine, *New Worlds*. This anthology was essentially a best of *New Worlds* effort, and it included five poems that had appeared in *New World*. For once the publisher apparently refrained from deleting poems. The book had been published earlier in England.

Bill Butler: "The first gorilla on the moon"
John Clark: "Saint 505"
Michael Hamburger: "Report on a supermarket"

George Macbeth: "Silver Needle"
Peter Redgrove: "The idea of entropy at Maenporth Beach"

Holding Your Eight Hands

Edited by Edward Lucie-Smith. Garden City, NY: Doubleday & Co., 1969.

Holding Your Eight Hands is a milestone in the history of science fiction and speculative poetry. The book has been the only collection of its kind published by a major American commercial house. In fact, there is a folklore tradition that it is one of the few poetry collections published by Doubleday that made enough to cover its costs.

The collection is a reprint of an English anthology of speculative rather than science fiction poetry, that is, poems that talk about the future and science but spoken in the language of mainstream literature rather than in traditional genre science fiction.

There are a few names famliar to science fiction fans in this work, such as Brian Aldiss, John Brunner, C. S. Lewis, John Sladek, and surprisingly H. P. Lovecraft. Some of the other poets such as Peter Redgrove and D. M. Thomas also had minor reputations in this country because of their work in *New Worlds*. In fact, the anthology has often been described as a collection of *New Worlds* poetry. This is not completely accurate. Rather, it was a collection of the type of poetry that was appearing in *New Worlds*, and some of the poems did appear in that magazine.

Since its appearance the anthology has often been touted as a seminal collection that other anthology editors ought to emulate. Some of the poems appearing in *Holding Your Eight Hands* were reprinted in other anthologies.

Brian W. Aldiss: "Progression of the Species"
Michael Benedikt: "A Beloved Head"
Asa Benveniste: "The Gardeners"
D. M. Black: "My Species," "The Basilisk"
John Brunner: "Citizen Bacillus," "To Myself on the Occasion of My
    Twenty-first Century"
John Ciardi: "A Magus"
Barry Cole: "An End to Complacency," "The Men Are Coming
    Back!"
John Robert Colombo: "Frankenstein"

Robert Conquest: "Far Out," "The Golden Age"

John Cotton: "Report Back"

Thomas M. Disch: "A Vacation on Earth," "Narcissus," "The Day Euterpe Died"

Mike Evans: "Mushrooms," "We'll All Be Spacemen Before We Die"

Ruth Fainlight: "A Report"

John Fairfax: "Beyond Astronaut"

Anthony Haden-Guest: "How the Consolations of Philosophy Worked Out in Actual Practice"

John Heath-Stubbs: "From an Ecclesiastical Chronicle"

Adrian Henri: "Galactic Lovepoem," "Universes"

Ted Hughes: "Ghost Crabs"

Ronald Johnson: "The Invaders"

David Kilburn: "Weather Forecast"

Kenneth Koch: "The Artist"

Ruth Lechtliner: "A Winter's Tale"

C. S. Lewis: "An Expostulation"

H. P. Lovecraft: "Harbour Whistles," "Nyarlathotep"

Edward Lucie-Smith: "Afterwards," "In the Future"

George Macbeth: "Bedtime Story," "Circe Undersea," "Mother Superior," "The Crab-Apple Crisis"

Edwin Morgan: "From the Domain of Arnheim," "In Sobieski's Shield"

Jeff Nuttall: "Poem"

Kenneth Patchen: "Wouldn't You After a Jaunt of 964,000,000,000,000 Million Miles?"

Brian Patten: "A Small Dragon," "Perhaps Where He Is Only Loving Rockets Can Land"

Peter Porter: "To Start a Controversey," "Your Attention Please"

Tom Raworth: "Ah the Poetry of Miss Parrot's Feet Demonstrating the Tango"

Peter Redgrove: "Mr. Waterman," "The Wizard's New Meeting"

John Sladek: "Love Nest," "The Treasure of the Haunted Rambler"

D. M. Thomas: "Missionary," "The Head-Rape," Tithonus"

Jonathan Williams: "Everybody's Homesick Soldier Boy"

Operation: Phantasy

Edited by Donald A. Wollheim. Rego Park, NY: The Phantagraphic Press, 1967.

Donald Wollheim is one of the leading editors in the science fiction and fantasy field. Currently he is the publisher of the imprint that bears his initials, DAW Books. Before that he was the science fiction editor at Ace, edited several short-lived science fiction magazines, and has put together numerous anthologies.

During the 1930s he was the publisher/editor of *The Phantagraph*, which was a short-lived fanzine or amateur magazine. Nevertheless, it featured a considerable body of work by major writers like H. P. Lovecraft, Frederick Pohl, and James Blish. Much of this work was poetry, and this anthology represents a good sampling of the kind of poetry that was being published in science fiction and horror pulp magazines of the period. The language was overblown, and the sentiments were perhaps too obvious for contemporary tastes. However, there was a sincerity and vision behind these poems that allow them to transcend their garishness.

James Blish: "Contrast"
Graham Conway: "Innocence"
August W. Derleth: "Only Deserted . . ."
Robert E. Howard: "Song at Midnight"
Cyril Kornbluth: "Chant of The Black Magicians," "Segment"
Henry Kuttner: "The Sunken Towers"
H. P. Lovecraft: "Harbour Whistles"
Robert Lowndes: "Fateful Hour," "Quarry"
A. Merritt: "Old Trinity Churchyard (5 A.M. Spring)"
John B. Michel: "The Unconquerable Fire"
Frederik Pohl: "Versiflage"
F. Stanislaus Prosody: "Jump-out-of-Bed"
Clark Ashton Smith: "The Memnons of the Night"

Poly

Edited by Lee Ballentine. Mountain View, CA: The Ocean View Press, 1989.

Poly is the first original anthology published by the Ocean View Press, which is the first commercial publishing firm that has made a commitment to publishing modern, speculative science fiction poetry.

While most of the material represented is poetry, there are a few pieces of prose and nonfiction scattered through the body of the work. It is a welcome turnabout; one usually found poetry scattered through the body of prose anthologies.

In his introduction, the editor, Lee Ballentine, makes the point that this is an anthology of speculative rather than science fiction poetry. From his perspective the difference between speculative and science fiction poetry is that speculative poetry talks about the future and science without reference to traditional science fiction themes and motifs.

I do not find this to be a significant difference. Science fiction writers both in prose and poetry have been constantly redefining the nature of science fiction literature almost as soon as it was defined and perceived as a distinct and separate genre. The result is that major science fiction work has nearly the same values and perspectives as speculative prose and poetry written by mainstream writers. Indeed mainstream writers have increasingly been adopting the canons and perspectives of science fiction. There are no longer two separate paths in this field.

This point is borne out by the fact that this anthology contains poetry by both genre poets who are strongly identified with science fiction such as Ray Bradbury, Jonathan Post, and David R. Bunch, and poets who can be described as mainstream speculative writers, like Al Zolynas, Michael Hamburger, and Peter Redgrove. It is ironic that *Poly* represents a refutation to the premise of Ballentine's introduction.

> Vance Aandahl: "Owleaters"
> Diane Ackerman: "Portrait Without Pose," "Transition," "The White Hypnosis"
> Ivan Arguelles: "Drum," "A History of the Dream," "In the Valley of the Pharaoh of the Shadow," "Wondering What Heaven Sounds Like After Death"
> Hans Arp: "Instead of Maps (Hans Arp in Heaven)," "Poem"
> Lee Ballentine: "Six Feathers of Aleron," "Trilby," "Ventriloquism"
> Lee Ballentine and Andrew Joron: "The Fate of Polyphemus"
> Lee Ballentine and Kathryn Rantala: "Clonehouse," "Hawk," "The Incense Salesman," "Poly," "Stars"
> Douglas Barbour: "These For Those From Whom," "Words, Perhaps, for Music"
> Alberto Blanco: "A Transparent Kingdom"

Bruce Boston: "Intersteller Tract," "No Longer the Stars," "Of Time and the Sideral Shore," "When Silver Plums Fall"

Ray Bradbury: "To Ireland No More"

David R. Bunch: "The Heartacher and the Warehouseman"

Andrew Darlington: "Against Heliocentricity," "Copenicus, City of the Dead," "Eyes Dreaming of Moscow," "I Can't Quite Remember the Re-Creation of the World," "The Mooncalf Pastures," "The Wave-Particle Paradox,"

Peter Dillingham: "The Antediluvian," "Black Holes & Hologramarye," "Cloud Skier," "Psi-Rec/Flying White," "Untitled Poems"

Tom Disch: "Richard Andsoforth"

Tom Disch and David Lehman: "Six Times Six, Plus Three, Times Four, in Five Seventy-Nine"

Jack Foley: "Assassin," "Certainty," "From Letters: Collage Poems," "The Visit"

Robert Frazier: "A Fractal Pattern," "A Measure of Light," "Three Scientific Love Poems"

David Gasceyne: "Procession to the Private Sector"

Oscar Hahn: "Vision of Hiroshima"

Michael Hamburger: "On Duty," "Postscript"

Andrew Joron: "Beacon," "Breaking into the Crystal Text," "Flats," "Post-Historic Pastorale," "Two Walkers Across the Time"

Mark Laba: "Card #27"

David Lunde: "Limits," "Looking Backward," "Monad for Jacques Monod," "Nuclear Winter"

Edward Mycue: "Threshold to a Far Distance"

Jonathan Post: "Catalyst," "The Fall of the City," "Mnemosyne's Entrenchment," "Sweet Radium"

Peter Redgrove: "Ascension," "Grand Buveur VIII," "The Horse and the Aphid," "In the Studio," "The Power," "Process," "Quick Air," "Vibes"

Mark Rich: "To the Colony"

Edouard Roditi: "The Advantages of Habit," "Bottled Time," "A Busy Nightlife," "A Dream of the Timeless World," "A History Lesson," "Meditation on a Worm's Life," "Of Politics and the Weather"

Horacio Salas: "Evil Eye"

John Oliver Simon: "Cerro De La Estrella," "Malinalco," "The Perfect Traveller"

Steve Rasnic Tem: "Looking Back on Apollo"

Georg Traki: "Decline," "Lament"
Yves Troendle: "Moon"
Tristan Tzara: "Great Complaint Against My Obscurity!!!"
    "Midnight Salts," "Optimism Unveiled," "Precise," "Yellow
    Cold"
Nanos Valaoritis: "Poem Unlimited"
Gene Van Troyer: "The Myth of the Man at the Center"
Al Zolynas: "My Mother and the Wheel of Fire"

The Pournelle Anthologies

Black Holes, *edited by Jerry E. Pournelle. New York: Fawcett Crest Books, 1975.*

The Endless Frontier, *edited by Jerry E. Pournelle and John F. Carr. New York: Ace Books, Vol. I (1979); Vol. II (1982).*

There Will Be War, *edited by Jerry E. Pournelle and John Carr. New York: Tor Books, Vol. I (1983); Vol. II (1984); Vol. III (1984); Vol. IV (1985); Vol. V (1986); Vol. VI (1987).*

Hard science fiction novelist Jerry Pournelle has been involved in several science fiction anthology projects since 1975. They are single-theme anthologies that use original and previously published material. His efforts remain one of the few ongoing commercial book publications for science fiction poetry.

Pournelle has a well-deserved reputation as a writer of popular but stereotypical, action-oriented science fiction, particularly military science fiction. Yet, he uses original science fiction poetry from writers whose work can be considered indifferent or even hostile to the values embodied in military science fiction. He has recently published poems by Frazier, Tem, Dillingham, and Post, who reject the values of military science fiction. His editorial policy places literary quality above political correctness, an expression of his own stubborn streak of independence.

Black Holes
Michael Bishop: "For the Lady of a Physicist"
Peter Dillingham: "Cygnus X-1," "The Salesman Who Fell from
    Grace with the Universe"

Endless Frontiers
Vol. I
Peter Dillingham: "House"

Vol. II
Judith R. Conly: "Songs of a Spacefarer"
Peter Dillingham: "Psi-Rec: Of Anabasis and Bivouac, the Swarm Cantor"
Robert A. Frazier: "The High-Lifter Trilogy"
Helene Knox: "Elegy," "Inner Space," "NASA"

There Will Be War
Vol. I
Joe Haldeman: "Saul's Death: Two Sestinas"
Rudyard Kipling: "The Widow's Party"
Jonathan V. Post: "Two Poems"

Vol. II
Robert Frazier: "Forbidden Lines"
Steve Rasnic Tem: "Two Poems"

Vol. III
Peter Dillingham: "Psi-Rec: Of Sword and Sitar, the War Without"
Rudyard Kipling: "The Earthen"

Vol. IV
G. K. Chesterton: "Lepanto"
Rudyard Kipling: "MacDonough's Song"

Vol. V
A. E. Houseman: "Three Poems"
Rudyard Kipling: "Ford O'Kabul River"

Vol. VI
Peter Dillingham: "Psi-Rec: Priest of Roses, Paladin of Swords, the War Within"
Dan Duncan: "Harmonica Song"
Robert Frazier: "Encased in the Amber of Probabilities"
Gregory Nicoll: "Galileo Saw the Truth"
Unknown: "Abduliah Bulbul Amir"

Rhysling Anthologies

The 1983 Rhysling Anthology, *edited by Robert Frazier. Los Angeles: Science Fiction Poetry Association, 1983.*
The 1984 Rhysling Anthology, *edited by Robert Frazier. Sun Valley, CA: Science Fiction Poetry Association, 1984.*
The 1985 Rhysling Anthology, *edited by Bruce Boston. Berkeley, CA: Science Fiction Poetry Association, 1985.*
The 1986 Rhysling Anthology, *edited by Bruce Boston. Berkeley, CA: Science Fiction Poetry Association, 1986.*
The 1987 Rhysling Anthology, *edited by Bruce Boston. Berkeley, CA: Science Fiction Poetry Association, 1987.*
The 1988 Rhysling Anthology, *edited by Chuck and Sue Rothman. Schenectady, NY: Science Fiction Poetry Association, 1988.*

These anthologies are compilations of the nominees for the Rhysling, the annual award for the best in Long and Short Poetry given by the Science Fiction Poetry Association. Previously nominees were published in annual Rhysling issues of *Star*Line*, though not all Rhysling nominees were reprinted due to copyright and other problems. This anthology series informally plays the role of the year's best in science fiction, fantasy, and horror poetry. It also shows the broad range of sources that publish genre poetry and the knack of professional poets for finding them. For example, in the 1986 Rhysling volume, all the poems except for one came from either newsstand or small-press genre sources. Only five out of the twenty-three poems appeared originally in newsstand science fiction magazines, mostly *Isaac Asimov.*

The anthologies series, like Frazier's *Burning with a Vision,* is a clear statement that poetry has become a part of American science fiction. However, since the vast majority of the nominees come from small-press sources within the genre, it reconfirms the idea that small-press publications represent the leading edge in poetry, a fact that is true in science fiction, fantasy, and horror as it is in mainstream literature.

1978
Duane Ackerson: "DNA," "The Starman"
Isaac Asimov: "Science Fiction Convention"
Michael Bishop: "Postcards to Athena"
Peter Dillingham: "Sweet Birds of Youth Trilogy"
Sonya Dorman: "Corruption of Metals"

Jo Ann Harper: "Feminine Demystification"
Andrew Joron: "Asleep in the Arms of Mother Night"
Frank Belknap Long: "The Marriage of Sir John de Mandeville"
Kathryn Rantala: "Voices"
Walter Shedlofsky: "Comrades brave, space beckons" (untitled),
    "Taffy Was a Spaceman"
Gene Wolfe: "The Computer Iterates the Greater Trumps"

1979
Duane Ackerson: "Fatalities"
Jack Anderson: "The Lost Space Ship"
Michael Bishop: "For the Lady of a Physicist"
John Bredon: "Storybooks and Treasure Maps"
Edward Bryant: "Winslow Crater"
Michael Carlson: "Deep Space Anthology"
Russell Edson: "Monkey Dinner"
Robert Frazier: "I, Flightless Peregrine," "A Peregrine Fantasy"
Adam Hammer: "Sailing Away"
Kathryn Rantala: "Harmoniums"

1980
Duane Ackerson: "After," "Stars, Crucified on Their Limbs of
    Light"
Bruce Boston: "If Gravity Were Like Weather"
Dave Calder: "Spaceman," "We Came in Peace for All Mankind"
Robert Frazier: "Encased in the Amber of Eternity"
Andrew Joron: "The Sonic Flowerfall of Primes"
Ursula K. LeGuin: "Siva And Kama"
Peter Payack: "The Migration of Darkness"
Neal Wilgus: "Metamorphosis"

1981
Peter Dillingham: "holovision/20-20"
Tom Disch: "On Science Fiction"
Raymond DiZazzo: "Cookers"
Ken Duffin: "Meeting Place"
Suzette Haden Elgin: "Lines on Looking into the Los Angeles ..."
Steve Eng: "Flaming Rose"
Frederico Licsi Espino: "Bionic Adam"
Janet Fox: "The teddybear that used" (untitled)
Stephen Gresham: "The Mooneyes of Dog Sunday"

Vicki Ann Heydron: "The Sacrifice"
F. Gwynplaine MacIntyre: "Improbable Estiary: The Centaur"
Frederick J. Mayer: "Dead"
Steven Edward McDonald: "On Our Holidays"
Steve Rasnic Tem: "The Landed Gentry"
Gene Van Troyer: "Gonna Laugh Dem Rollin Bones"
Chad Walsh: "The First Two Men (?) From Outer Space"
Neal Wilgus: "Endtime Rag"
Paul Edwin Zimmer: "The Complaint of Agni"

1982
Ray DiZazzo: "On the Speed of Sight"
Terry Garey: "The Grove"
Albert Goldbarth: "Saucer Station, Monday-Friday"
Elissa L. A. Hamilton: "Ybba"
Andrew Joron and Robert Frazier: "Their terminals have said . . ."
    (untitled)
Ursula K. LeGuin: "The Well of Baln"
Adrienne Marcus: "Paper Clocks"
Marge Piercy: "Absolute Zero in the Brain"
Kathryn Rantala: "Noah at Sea," "Voyager IV"
Gene Van Troyer and Robert Frazier: "The Starfarers"

1983
Erland Anderson: "Against the Anniversary of Our Extinction"
Bruce Boston: "Human Remains"
Adam Cornford: "Your Time and You"
Sonya Dorman: "Star Songs"
Elissa L. A. Hamilton: "The Last Planetarium Convention"
Andrew Joron: "The Hunter: 20,000 A.D."
Alan P. Lightman: "In Computers"
Nancy Springer: "The Wolf Girl Speaks"
Steve Rasnic Tem: "Syrup"
Lewis Turco: "The Stone: An Indian Legend"
Gene Van Troyer: "Three Views of the Cosmic Ballet"
Jane Yolen: "Neptune Rising"

1984
Bruce Boston: "The FTL Addict Fixes"
Adam Cornford: "The Outer Limits"
Helen Ehrlich: "Two Sonnets"

Laura Farges: "The Island of Geological Time"
Joe W. Haldeman: "Saul's Death: Two Sestinas"
Andrew Joron: "The Webbed Axis"
Elissa Malcohn: "Wings"
Ed Orr: "Accountability"
David Piercy: "When Again the Glass Flutes Bloom"
Ruth Lisa Schechter: "Recognition of the Tigers"

1985
Hope Athearn: "The Twenty-Fifth"
Michael Bishop: "Independence Day Forever"
Bruce Boston: "For Spacers Snarled in the Hair of Comets"
Anne Braude: "Launcelot in Winter"
Siv Cedering: "A Letter from Caroline Herschel"
Helen Ehrlich: "For Alfred, Lord Tennyson"
Bill Hotchkiss: "Audible Lithography"
Andrew Joron and Robert Frazier: "Homonid Voices"
Suzanne Lummis: "How It All Began"
David Lunde: "The Still Point"
Chuck Oliveros: "The Man Who Left Us Behind"
Jonathan V. Post: "The Problem of Pain"

1986
Bruce Boston: "Evolution of the Death Murals"
Michael R. Collings: "The Last Pastoral," "Sputnik"
Andrew Darlington: "The Flight in the Cave of the
     Moonbutchers/the Mooncalf"
Ron Ellis: "Car Radio," "Neutrino Mantra"
Steve Eng: "Bardicide"
Michael Finley: "The Man in the Air"
B. Buckley Finnegan: "Orbiting Structure"
Robert Frazier: "Perception Barriers"
Rochelle Lynn Holt: "Without Dreams"
Andrew Joron: "Shipwrecked on Destiny Five"
Thomas Ligotti: "One Thousand Painful Variations Performed upon
     Divers Creatures Undergoing the Treatment of Dr. Moreau,
     Humanist"
Elissa Malcohn: "Pantoum for a Switched Identity"
Richard McMullen: "Dracula's Dentist"
Susan Palwick: "The Neighbor's Wife"
Jonathan V. Post: "To the Stars: Love Hypertext"

Ken Poyner: "The Last Day"
Mark Rich: "Post"
Peter Viereck: "Rogue"
t. Winter-Damon: "Flickering Blue Extreme"
Jane Yolen: "Into the Wood"

1987

Ivan Arguelles: "Autoincineration of the Right Stuff"
Ruth Berman: "Open-Ended Universe"
Bruce Boston: "Uroboros"
Steve Bowkett: "Moonwatcher"
S. R. Compton: "Retreat"
Keith Allen Daniels: "My Eyes My Eyes Are Melting"
Andrew Darlington: "Hiroshima Mon Amour/Radical Kisses"
Harry Davidov: "The Wizard of the Word"
James S. Dorr: "A Neo-Canterbury Tale: The Hog Driver's Tale"
Robert Frazier: "Tourist Spots for Time Travelers," "The Veneers of
    Sleep"
David Lunde: "Limits"
Jonathan V. Post: "Before the Big Bang"
John Calvin Rezmerski: "A Dream of Heredity"
David M. Skov: "Aversion"
W. Gregory Stewart: "Daedalus"
Jane Yolen: "The Making of Dragons"

1988

Gregory Benford: "Bleak Velocities"
Bruce Boston: "Interstellar Tract," "The Nightmare Collector"
Jack Butler: "Kybernetikos," "The Spider"
Marcia Cohee: "Incubus"
S. R. Compton: "And at That Moment . . . ," The Drowners"
Denise Dumars: "I Am Myself — What Others Said Was True"
Roger Dutcher and Robert Frazier: "Nazca Lines"
Suzette Haden Elgin: "Rocky Road to Hoe"
Ron Ellis: "Wind Gauge"
Robert Frazier: "Tracking Through the Mutant Rain Forest"
Thomas Glave: "Landscape in Black"
Albert Goldbarth: "The Way the Novel Functions"
John Grey: "Chinese Food, That Last Time"
Eileen Kernaghan: "Tales from the Holographic Woods"
Sandra Lindow: "What to Do with a Dead Dragon"

Hank Mannheimer: "Col. Barry Fields (Ret.)"
Paul Merchant: "from A LIFE OF COPERNICUS"
John Calvin Rezmerski: "Challengers"
Mark Rich: "Descent," "On Escaping"
Tom Riley: "Ruby Angels"
Marilyn Shea: "OM"
Lucius Shepard: "White Trains"
Steve Sneyd: "On the Line of the Ecliptic"

Songs from Unsung Worlds

Edited by Bonnie Bilyeu Gordon. Boston, MA: Birkhauser, 1985.

While commercially published anthologies of poems about science are fairly common in England, this is one of few such efforts appearing in America. The anthology came about through the efforts of the editors of *Science*, the official magazine of the American Association for the Advancement of Science. The editors noted the strong, positive reception that poetry has received in its pages. However, this collection is not a "Best Of" from *Science*'s pages. Rather it was a successful attempt to give the reader an overview of the whole field of science poetry. The majority of the poems came from sources other than *Science*. The sources included science fiction magazines, single-author collections, and major literary magazines.

The anthology is divided into four sections. The first contains poems about scientists and their work, the second, poems about natural phenomena, the third, poems that use the language of science as metaphor for other themes, and the fourth, poems that satirize science.

Dannie Abse: "The Stethoscope"
Diane Ackerman: "Ice Dragons," "Ode to the Alien," "St. Augustine
　　Contemplating the Bust of Einstein," "Space Shuttle"
A. R. Ammons: "80-Proof," "Rivulose," "Time's Times Again"
W. H. Auden: "Moon Landing," "Progress," "The Question,"
　　"Unpredictable but Providential"
Lois Bassen: "Brain Coral"
Marvin Bell: "The Parents of Psychotic Children"
Michael Benedikt: "Of How Scientists Are Often Ahead of Others
　　in Thinking While the Average Man Lags Behind; and How
　　the Economist (Who Can Only Follow in the Footsteps of the

Average Man Looking for Clues to the Future) Remains
Thoroughly Out of It," "The Future," "The Life of Particles"
Jody Bolz: "Migration as a Passage in Time"
Olga Broumas: "from Backgammon"
Carol Burbank: "Call to Order," "Surgery"
Michael Cadnum: "Skull of a Neandertal"
Siv Cedering: "A Letter from Caroline Herschel (1750–1848),"
"Letter from the Astronomers"
Amy Clampitt: "Amphibian," "Berceuse," "Camouflage," "The
Cormorant in Its Element," "A Curfew: December 13, 1981"
Michael Collier: "Counting"
e. e. cummings: "La Guerre"
Ann Darr: "Whatever It Was I Was Saving for My Old Age"
Lucille Day: "Neural Folds," "Self-Portrait with Hand
Microscope," "Tumor"
Emily Dickinson: "Arcturus is his other name, -"
Patric Dickinson: "Jodrell Bank"
Annie Dillard: "Light in the Open Air," "The Windy Planet"
R.H.W. Dillard: "How Copernicus Stopped the Sun," "How
Einstein Started It Up Again"
John Donne: "Love's Alchemy"
Ann Downer: "Koko"
Helen Ehrlich: "Two Sonnets"
Loren Eisley: "The Spider," Winter Sign"
Laura Fargas: "The Island of Geological Time," "Natural History,"
"Roeschach"
Carrol B. Fleming: "Boundaries"
Robert Frazier: "Marie Curie Contemplating the Role of Women
Scientists in the Glow of a Beaker," "The Supremacy of
Bacteria," "Telephone Ghosts"
Martin Galvin: "Doorman"
Johann Wolfgang von Goethe: "Entoptic Colors," "True Enough: To
the Physicist (1820)"
John Haines: "Little Cosmic Dust Poem"
Carolin Breese Hall: "Chicken Soup Therapy: Its Made of Action"
Roald Hoffman: "Finnair Fragment," "From a Rise of Land to the
Sea"
Miroslav Holub: "Brief Reflections on the Insect," "Evening in a
Lab," "Hominization," "Newborn Baby," "Poem Technology,"
"Teaching about Arthropods," "Teeth," "Wings," "Zito the
Magician"

Ann Rae Jonas: "The Cat in the Box," "The Causes of Color"
Josie Kearns: "The Planets Line Up for a Demonstration"
Galway Kinnell: "The Fundamental Project of Technology"
Maxine Kumin: "Getting Through"
David Lehman: "Perpetual Motion"
Alan P. Lightman: "First Rainfall," "In Computers"
Katharine Auchincloss Lorr: "The Beekeeper's Dream," "Peking
    Man, Raining"
Cynthia MacDonald: "Dr. Dimity Is Forced to Complain," "Dr.
    Dimity Lectures on Unusual Cases"
Joseph Matuzak: "Nystagmus"
David McAleavey: "At the Scenic Drive-in," "Gate"
Heather McHugh: "Down, Down, Down," "A Physics"
Peter Meinke: "Hermann Ludwig Ferdinand Von Helmholtz,"
    "Mendel's Law"
Robert Mezey: "In This Life," "Song"
G. F. Montgomery: "Graham Bell and the Photophone"
Richard Moore: "The Swarm"
Robert Morgan: "Brevard Fault," "Jutaculla Rock," "Thermometer
    Wine"
Howard Nemerov: "The Weather of the World"
John Frederick Nims: "The Observatory Ode"
J. Robert Oppenheimer: "Crossing"
David Palmer: "Plato Instructs a Midwest Farmer"
Anselm Parlatore: "Accommodation," "Although in a Crystal,"
    "Cancer Research," "Famly Chronicle," "Lovely Girls with
    Flounders on a Starry Night"
Linda Pastan: "Waiting for E. gularis"
Anne S. Perlman: "At Liberty," "The Specialist," "Viking 1 on Mars
    — July 20, 1976"
Jonathan V. Post: "Footnote to Feynman"
Bin Ramke: "The Monkish Mind of the Speculative Physicist"
Danny Rendleman: "Toward a Theory of Instruction"
David St. John: "Two Sorrows," "Wavelength"
Robert Sargent: "The Concept of Force"
Timothy Sheehan: "At Camino," "Eclipse"
Judith Skillman: "Waiting"
Myra Sklarew: "Hieroglyphic," "The Origin of Species"
Gary Snyder: "Once Only," "Toward Climax"
William Stafford: "A Message from Space," "Ways of
    Seeing"

George Starbuck: "Magnificat in Transit from the Toledo Airport,"
  "Pit Viper," "The Universe Is Closed and has REMs"
Wallace Stevens: "Connoisseur of Chaos"
Arthur Stewart: "Fossils"
May Swenson: "The Cross Spider," "Orbiter 5 Shows How Earth
  Looks from the Moon," "The Universe"
David Wagoner: "In Distress," "My Physics Teacher"
Diane Wakoski: "For Whitman"
Walt Whitman: "When I Heard the Learn'd Astronomer"
Richard Wilbur: "Epistemology"
Gary Young: "The Doctor Rebuilds a Hand," "Equinox," "Tornado
  Watch, Bloomington, Indiana"

The Umbral Anthology of Science Fiction Poetry

Edited by Steve Rasnic Tem. Denver: Umbral Press, 1982.

In the late 1970s and early 1980s Tem published an occasional
speculative poetry magazine called *Umbral. The Umbral Anthology*
was his last publishing effort before he started a successful career as a
full-time writer of science fiction and horror.

Despite the anthology's title, the collection was oriented toward
speculative rather than purely science fiction poetry. In fact several of
the poems that appeared in *Holding Your Eight Hands* were reprinted
in this work. More important, the anthology featured the work of such
mainstream poets as Marge Piercy and Roswell Spafford, writers who
had never before been associated with science fiction. The anthology
represented the first major appearance of Steven Sneyd, an English poet
whose appearances until that time in America had been limited to
small-press magazines.

The Umbral Anthology was not the first independently published
science fiction poetry anthology. However, it was a professional
publication that had some limited access to regular book distribution
channels.

Diane Ackerman: "Lady Faustus"
Duane Ackerson: "Science Fiction Story," "The Starman"
Brian Aldiss: "Progression of the Species"
Dick Allen: "Can to Ten (from ANON)," "Hyperspace," "The
  Perpetual Motion Machine," "Theory of the Alternate
  Universe," "To an Astronaut.."

Jack Anderson: "Flying Saucers Have Landed . . ." "Second Sight,"
    "The Lost Space Ship," "The Mysterious Sound"
Margaret Atwood: "Speeches for Dr. Frankenstein"
Marvin Bell: "Remembering a Window"
Gregory Benford: "Lust"
Judith Berke: "Future Baby," "Us"
Michael Bishop: "Among the Hominids at Olduvai," "ITH-
    CORO," "Vultures"
Ray Bradbury: "The Beast upon the Wire"
David R. Bunch: "(Hope) (Ambition) (Anticipation)," "Practicing"
Melissa Cannon: "Planet of Voices: Initiation"
Andrew Darlington: "A Plague of Dreamers After the Raid,"
    "Circular Error Probability," "Full Frontal Jazz"
Tom Disch: "Alternate Universe I, II, III," "Apollo 14," "On Science
    Fiction," "Song of Myself," "The Growth of the Church," "The
    Turtle's Dream," "The Vegetables"
Sonya Dorman: "Corruption of Metals," "End of the Day," "Once in
    a Blue Moon," "The Child Dreams," "View from the Moon
    Station," "Winter City"
Russell Edson: "A Machine," "Counting Sheep," "The Tool"
Barbara Eve: "The Gymnasium"
Gary Fincke: "Balloon Song," "Gravity Failing," "Parade Test,"
    "The Changing OC," "The Robot Guard"
Robert Frazier: "Black Ice," "Encased in the Amber of Death,"
    "Encased in the Amber of Eternity," "Encased in the Amber of
    Fate," "Mapping the Island in Images"
Barry Goldensohn: "The Returned Utopians"
Marilyn Hacker: "Nightsong," "Prayer for My Daughter"
H. R. Hays: "Invasion"
Cecil Helman: "The Landscape of Tin Statues"
Geof Hewitt: "At One with the Blue Night," "The Frozen Man"
William Heyen: "Machines to Kiss You Goodnight," "The Machine
    That Mends Birds' Nests," "The Machine That Puts You to
    Sleep," "The Machine That Treats Other Machines"
Christopher Howell: "The Beast of Lovimer County," "The Monster
    That Ate Sandusky"
Ted Hughes: "Ghost Crabs"
Mark Jarman: "From Another Planet"
Andrew Joron: "The Sonic Flowerfall of Primes,"' "The Tetrahedron
    Letters"
Weldon Kess: "The Coming of the Plague"

Ron Koertge: "The Blob"
Steve Kowit: "Home"
Judith Kroll: "Science Fiction Poem"
Ruth Lechtliner: "A Winter's Tale"
Archibald Macleish: "Epistle to Be Left in the Earth," "The End of the World"
Bruce McAllister: "First and Last Contact"
Frederick Morgan: "from A BOOK OF CHANGE, Part Three: II, VII, XVII," "The Promise"
Mary Tall Mountain: "The Last Wolf"
Peter Payack: "The Beginning of Things," "The Migration of Darkness," "The Origins of the Material World," "The Result of the Dig," "The Ultimate Party"
Marge Piercy: "Absolute Zero in the Brain," "The World in the Year 2000"
Craig Raine: "A Martian Sends a Postcard Home"
Kathryn Rantala: "The Second Collecting Mission," "Voices," "Wind"
James Reiss: "Small Thin Children Live in Flat Holes"
George Roberts: "déjà vu," "Poem," "Visitor"
Richard Schramm: "Letters from Another World," "The Calamity"
Jane Shore: "An Astronaut's Journal"
Joel Sloman: "The Astronaut of Waste"
Steve Sneyd: "An End to an Old Song," "Come One Come All," "In Case of Doubt, Ask," "Relief of the Lost Colony," "Sunset Strip," "Time Machine"
Roswell Spafford: "Leaving the Water," "Unlike"
William Stafford: "Storm Warning," "The Thought Machine"
James Tate: "The Immortals"
Steve Rasnic Tem: "The Hydrocephalic Ward," "The Swimmer"
D. M. Thomas: "A Dead Planet," "An Android," "Elegy for an Android," "Missionary," "S. F.," "The Head-Rape," "The Strait," "Tithonous," "Two Sonnets"
Bill Tremblay: "Parable of the Robot Poem," "To William Blake," "View from Atlantis"
Gene Van Troyer: "Three Views of the Cosmic Ballet"
David Wagoner: "The Man from the Top of the Mind"
James L. White: "Navajo Moon"
Miller Williams: "Problems in the Space-Time Continuum . . . ," "Story of a Memory and His Man," "We"

Vaughan Anthologies

Alternate Lives, *edited and published by Ralph E. Vaughan. Chula Vista, CA, 1986.*

Lost Lands, *edited and published by Ralph E. Vaughan, San Diego, CA, 1982.*

A Walk in the Dark, *edited and published by Ralph E. Vaughan. Chula Vista, CA, 1985.*

For the last several years, Ralph Vaughan has put together poetry anthologies of original and reprint material about specific science fiction and horror themes. *Alternate Lives* is about alternate universes; *Lost Lands* is about lost civilizations and races, and *A Walk in the Dark* is a general horror anthology about fear.

Vaughan's books look extremely crude, which makes them unattractive to some readers. The poems look as if Vaughan just splashed them on the page.

Vaughan has begun publishing single-author collections. He has already reprinted H. P. Lovecraft's *Fungi from Yuggoth* and plans a collection of poems by Duane Rimel, a 1930s fan who had some interesting poems appear in *Weird Tales*.

Alternate Lives
Larry Baukin: "Tourists"
Donna Buschmeier: "Epilogue," "Primitives"
Robert Frazier: "The Veneers of Sleep"
Robert Hall: "Reverie," "Revision 32"
Dwight E. Humphries: "Patrol"
Kim L. Neidigh: "Minor Alteration," "Pancake"
Walter Pokawanaka: "Hopi Dreams"
Tom Rentz: "Hall of Time"
Mark Rich: "Musings on a Minor Composer," "No Rousseau"
John B. Roseman: "Dallas"
John Saito: "Rings"
Christopher Lee Vaughan: "Illegal Books"
Ralph E. Vaughan: "Under Maybe Flags"
Kyle T. Zelachowski: "Fugi"

Lost Lands
Bruce Boston: "Green Sea"
August Derleth and Donald Wandrei: "Antarktos"

Janet Fox: "Golden Apples"
Scott E. Green: "The City Behind the Horizon"
Kim Herber: "Sea Escape"
Jerry Kobelski: "Rebirth"
Jon A. Marracott: "Merrika Dreams"
Jonathan V. Post: "Conquistador: Oblivion," "Violin of Night"
Frank Ramirez: "Reticentaur"
Tam Schact: "Cretean Bulls," "Egyptian Ways," "Mayan
    Nightfall," "several untitled Haikus"
Clark Ashton Smith: "Tolometh"
Jeff P. Swycaffer: "A.U.C."
Ralph E. Vaughan: "Devils," "Sri Lanka"
Leilah Wendell: "Escape"
Neal Wilgus: "Abandon Canyon," "Lost Land Regained"

A Walk in the Dark

Larry Baukin: "Baptism," "Devil's Food Cake," "The Interview,"
    "The Last Red Lobster," "The Tomb"
Jeanne M. Bezko: "Nightmares of the Beast"
Sharon Brondos: "Horror Stories"
Sonna Buschmeier: "Breaking Point," "Identity Crisis"
Lord Byron: "Darkness"
Margaret Flanagan Eicher: "The Arsonist," "The Last Appetite"
Michael Fantina: "The Demon Box," "Figurine," "The Griffin"
H. R. Felgenhauer: "People Who Walk in the Rain," "The Signal"
Janet Fox: "The Babysitter," "Little Cloth Doll"
Robert Frazier: "Video Phantasms"
Scott E. Green: "Dog on a Road," "Motel," "Slowly Rolling in
    Neutral"
Robert Hall: "(Life on) the Farm," "S.O.S."
Mike Handley: "i am afraid to open . . ." (untitled)
Randall Jarrell: "In Montecito"
Jeannie M. Leighton: "On the Beach II," "Voices in the Closet"
Elaine Lintzenich: "Demon Unexorcised"
Edward Mycue: "In the Valleys of the Alps"
John Phillips Palmer: "The Zombie Bride"
Zora Reeves: "Winds"
Duane Rimel: "Return," "The Worm"
Jessica Amanda Salmonson: "A Saint's Repose"
David Starkey: "Unborn Babes and Successful Suicides"
Steve Rasnic Tem: "The Changeling," "Into the Giant"

Richard Toelly: "Intruder"

Christopher Lee Vaughan: "Monsters in the Cellar"

R. E. Vaughan: "Aztec Dreams," "Hunger," "Life Through Channels," "Lithic Dog," "On the Bus"

t. Winter-Damon: "Flickering Blue Extreme," "Visitations of the Mermaid's Inn," "Maniak Upstairs," "Meat Cleaver"

Historical Anthologies

Annual Science Fiction Anthology Series

Edited by Judith Merrill

SF: 57 The Year's Greatest Science Fiction and Fantasy. *New York: Gnome Press, 1957.*
The Year's Best SF — 5th Annual Edition. *New York: Dell, 1960.*
6th Annual Edition: The Year's Best SF. *New York: Dell, 1961.*
7th Annual Edition: The Year's Best SF. *New York: Dell, 1963.*
9th Annual Edition: The Year's Best SF. *New York: Dell, 1964.*
10th Annual Edition: The Year's Best SF. *New York: Dell, 1966.*
SF 12. *New York: Dell, 1968*

From 1956 until 1970 Judith Merrill edited an annual series of the year's best in science fiction. Unlike other editors, she looked to mainstream markets for material or poetry to buy. The issues listed above were volumes that included poetry. The seventh edition was significant because it reprinted poetry mostly from mainstream sources rather than science fiction magazines. Toward the end of the anthology series Merrill became a strong advocate of the New Wave speculative fiction and poetry being published in British *New Worlds*. The eleventh and twelfth volumes each had a poem that originally had appeared in *New Worlds*. This probably constituted the first appearances of *New Worlds* poetry on the American side of the Atlantic. There were other poems in these volumes from mainstream sources that were close in spirit and approach to *New World* poetry.

Asimov Magazine Anthology (series)

Asimov's Choice: Astronauts & Androids, *edited by George Scithers. New York: Davis Publications, 1977.*

Asimov's Choice: Dark Stars & Dragons, *edited by George Scithers. New York: Davis Publications, 1977.*

Isaac Asimov's Aliens & Outworlders, *edited by Shawna McCarthy. New York: Davis Publicationss, 1983.*

Isaac Asimov's Science Fiction Anthology, *Vol. 5, edited by George Scithers. New York: Davis Publicationss, 1982.*

Isaac Asimov's Space of Her Own, *edited by Shawna McCarthy. New York: Davis Publicationss, 1983.*

Isaac Asimov's Wonders of the World, *edited by Kathleen Moloney and Shawna McCarthy. New York: Davis Publicationss, 1982.*

These anthologies are "Best Of" prose and poetry that had appeared in *Isaac Asimov's Science Fiction Magazine*. Most of the poetry reprinted is light, humorous verse. Probably for that reason several of the major poets published in the magazine do not appear in these volumes. An exception was F. Gwynplaine MacIntyre whose output as a poet leaned toward the humorous. The anthologies were published in a digest magazine format and were usually found in magazine sections of book stores.

The Best from Fantasy and Science Fiction Series

The Best from Fantasy and Science Fiction 3, *edited by Anthony Boucher and Francis McComas. Garden City, NY: Doubleday & Co., 1954.*

The Best from Fantasy and Science Fiction 4, *edited by Anthony Boucher. Garden City, NY: Doubleday & Co., 1955.*

The Best from Fantasy and Science Fiction 5, *edited by Anthony Boucher. Garden City, NY: Doubleday & Co., 1956.*

The Best from Fantasy and Science Fiction 6, *edited by Anthony Boucher. Garden City, NY: Doubleday & Co., 1957.*

The Best from Fantasy and Science Fiction 7, *edited by Anthony Boucher. Garden City, NY: Doubleday & Co., 1958.*

The Best from Fantasy and Science Fiction 8, *edited by Anthony Boucher. Garden City, NY: Doubleday & Co., 1959.*

The Best from Fantasy and Science Fiction 9, *edited by Anthony Boucher. Garden City, NY: Doubleday & Co., 1960.*
The Best from Fantasy and Science Fiction 10, *edited by Robert P. Mills. Garden City, NY: Doubleday & Co., 1961.*
The Best from Fantasy and Science Fiction 11, *edited by Robert P. Mills. Garden City, NY: Doubleday & Co., 1962.*
The Best from Fantasy and Science Fiction 15, *edited by Edward L. Ferman, Jr. Garden City, NY: Doubleday & Co., 1966.*
The Best from Fantasy and Science Fiction 16, *edited by Edward L. Ferman, Jr. Garden City, NY: Doubleday & Co., 1967.*
The Best from Fantasy and Science Fiction, *22nd series, edited by Edward L. Ferman, Jr. Garden City, NY: Doubleday & Co., 1977.*
The Best from Fantasy and Science Fiction, *24th series, edited by Edward L. Ferman, Jr. New York: Charles Scribner's Sons, 1979.*

This was an annual anthology series of the year's best work appearing in the *Magazine of Fantasy and Science Fiction.* From 1954 to 1962 the annual featured poetry on a regular basis. Thereafter poetry appeared only sporadically. This was the only time during the 1950s and the early 1960s when science fiction and fantasy poetry regularly appeared in a mass-market format. Ironically, when these volumes were reprinted by Ace in paperback, most if not all the poems were deleted. While the poems appearing in the magazine were equally divided betwen horror, fantasy, and science fiction, the poems chosen to be reprinted were usually science fiction. There have been occasional one-shot anthologies of material appearing in the *Magazine of Fantasy and Science Fiction* that are not part of this series.

Best SF Series

Edited by Harry Harrison and Brian Aldiss

Best SF: 1968. *New York: Putnam, 1969.*
Best SF: 1969. *New York: Putnam, 1970.*
Best SF: 1971. *New York: Putnam, 1972.*
Best SF: 1972. *New York: Putnam, 1973.*
Best SF: 1973. *New York: Putnam, 1974.*
Best SF: 1974. *New York: Berkley Medallion, 1975.*

This annual anthology series was an attempt to sustain the spirit of the earlier Merrill anthologies, that is, reprinting prose and poetry that stretched and expanded the definition of science fiction. Much of the work came from mainstream, especially English, sources. Most of the poetry leaned toward speculative rather than science fiction poetry. For several American poets like Steven Utley, William Jon Watkins, and Duane Ackerson this series represented their first major appearance in a commercial work.

Best SF Stories from New Worlds 4

Edited by Michael Moorcock. New York: Berkley Medallion, 1969.

Moorcock, the editor of *New Worlds*, put together several volumes of *New Worlds* stories that was published by Berkley. This volume was the only one that had poetry and is significant in that it represented the first American commercial appearance of D. M. Thomas.

Fadiman's Mathematics Anthologies

Fantasia Mathematica, *edited by Clifton Fadiman. New York: Simon & Schuster, 1958.*
The Mathematical Magpie, *edited by Clifton Fadiman. New York: Simon & Schuster, 1962.*

These two anthologies edited by Clifton Fadiman were collections of stories and poetry about the science of mathematics. Most of the poetry was clever, witty, punnish pieces written by such mainstream poets as Christopher Morley, A. C. Hilton, Lewis Carroll, Edna St. Vincent Millay, Rachel Lindsay, A. E. Houseman, Samuel Butler, Carl

Sandburg, and even the occasional scientist such as George Gamow. However, a few science fiction writers had their work in the two volumes, including C. M. Kornbluth, Edgar Allan Poe, and Hilbert Schenck.

From *Unknown Worlds*

Edited by John W. Campbell, Jr. New York: Street & Smith, 1953.

During the late 1930s and early 1940s, the magazine *Unknown*, rival of *Weird Tales*, thrived. However, it focused on light fantasy in modern settings with tongue usually in cheek. This anthology was retrospective and had some of the poetry in the magazine.

Laughing Space

Edited by Isaac Asimov and Janet O. Jeppson. Boston: Houghton Mifflin, 1982.

Laughing Space, as its name implies, was an anthology about humorous science fiction. Much of the poetry in it was reprinted from the pages of *The Magazine of Fantasy and Science Fiction*. Surprisingly, few of the reprinted poems contain the insider jokes that only a true science fiction fan could appreciate. In most cases the humor is more ironic than belly laughs.

Main Stream Horror Anthologies

Something Strange, *edited by Marjorie B. Smiley, Mary Delores Jarman, and Domica Paterno. New York: Macmillan Publishing Co., 1967.*
Unknown Worlds, *edited by Lawana Trout. New York: Holt, Rinehart & Winston, 1969.*
Wolf's Complete Book of Terror, *edited by Leonard Wolf. New York: Clarkson N. Potter, Inc., 1979.*

These three anthologies featured horror, prose, and poetry by mainstream rather than genre writers. The language of the poems was the horror equivalent of speculative poetry. The language did not refer to genre references and images. Most of the poetry was nineteenth-century work, though there were more contemporary pieces such as Langston Hughes's "End," which appeared in the Wolf anthology, and May Swenson's "Southbound on the Freeway," which appeared in the Trout anthology.

The Man Who Called Himself Poe

Edited by Sam Moskowitz. Garden City, NY: Doubleday & Co., 1969.

This was a retrospective collection of prose and poetry about Edgar Allan Poe. Stories about Poe have always been a vigorous but small subgenre in American horror fiction.

The poems, however, are not narratives but tributes or reflections on Poe's career and life. Perhaps the most interesting is August Derleth's "Providence: Two Gentlemen at Midnight." It is an odd little poem that has the ghost of Poe meeting H. P. Lovecraft, the other great American horror writer. Derleth, of course, was Lovecraft's most famous protégé.

Of Men and Machines

Edited by Arthur O. Lewis, Jr. New York: E. P. Dutton & Co., 1963.

This prose and poetry anthology featured work concerning the relationship of people and technology, a major concern in genre science fiction. However, this anthology featured poetry by major American mainstream poets. In many but not all cases, the setting of the poems was in the future. Among the poets whose work appeared in the anthology were Robert Frost, Walt Whitman, Carl Sandberg, Stephen V. Benet, Stephen Crane, W. H. Auden, and e. e. cummings. The anthology is a reminder that "science fiction" themes have always been an important part of mainstream poetry, not just restricted to genre publications.

The Pulps

Edited by Tony Goodstone. New York: Chelsea House, 1970.

This coffee-table book reprinted prose and poetry that had appeared in the science fiction, fantasy, horror, adventure, and other pulp magazines that thrived during the 1920s, 1930s, and 1940s. All the poems reprinted were from horror sources.

Speculative Anthologies

Inside Information, *edited by Abbe Mowshowitz. Reading, MA: Addison-Wesley Publishing Co., 1977.*

Looking Ahead, *edited by D. and L. Allen. New York: Harcourt Brace Jovanovich, 1975.*

Man Unwept, *edited by Stephen V. Whalen and Stanley J. Cook. New York: McGraw-Hill Book Co., 1974.*

Science Fact/Fiction, *no editor listed. Glenview, IL: Scott Foresman & Co., 1974.*

Science Fiction, *no editor listed. Evanston, IL: McDougal, Littell & Co., 1973.*

Science Fiction: The Future, *edited by Dick Allen. New York: Harcourt Brace Jovanovich, 1971.*

Tomorrow, *edited by Alan L. Madsen. New York: Scholastic Book Service, 1973.*

These anthologies published science fiction prose and poetry that were particularly concerned with the future of human society. The reprinted material focused on the genre as a genre of ideas.

The poetry was almost entirely by mainstream writers who used non-genre language in their work. The writers represented included Anne Sexton, William Blake, William Yeats, Richard Brautigan (his "All Watched Over by Machines of Loving Grace" was in several anthologies), Mike Evans, William Faulkner, Dick Allen, Louis B. Salomon (his "Univac to Univac" was another reprint favorite), Robert Frost, William Stafford, Allen Ginsburg, Kenneth Koch, and Sylvia Plath. The few genre poets that did appear were writers like Tom Disch and D. M. Thomas who established their reputation in the pages of *New Worlds* in its "New Wave" form.

Star Trek: The New Voyages 2

Edited by Sandra Marshak and Myrna Culbreath. New York: Bantam Books, 1978.

There is a large segment of the science fiction fannish community devoted to the television and movie series "Star Trek." Countless fanzines published fiction, poetry, and articles about every possible permutation of the Star Trek Universe. This volume was part of a series that reprinted the best of this vast body of work in a commercial format and was the only volume that had any of the poetry.

Synergy

Edited by George Zebrowski. San Diego: Harcourt Brace Jovanovich. Vol. One (1987); Vol. Two (1988).

Since the 1960s there have been several series of original science fiction anthologies (*Orbit, New Dimensions, Universe*). Some occasionally published poetry. *Synergy* is a new series in this tradition. Its editor, George Zebrowski, plans to use poetry on a regular basis for the series. Poems by Frazier and Benford have already appeared as well as an article on the nature of science fiction poetry by Andrew Joron.

The purpose of the series is to encourage writers to write prose and poetry that is experimental in viewpoint and execution, in other words, to redefine the genre known as science fiction. This is a noble ideal and one that seems to be a particularly important goal for original science fiction anthology editors.

Zebrowski also edits the annual Nebula Award anthologies for the Science Fiction Writers of America. As editor he revived the practice of including Rhysling winners in the volumes, a practice first started by Joe Haldeman when he edited the Nebula anthologies.

Velocities Boxed Set

Edited by Andrew Joron. Mountain View, CA: Ocean View Press, 1988.

The Velocities Boxed Set is not an anthology. Rather, it is a re-release of the first five issues of *Velocities*, a magazine of speculative poetry published and edited by Andrew Joron. Joron himself is a leading poet in this field, and his own work vigorously avoids science fiction clichés while talking about the themes associated with science fiction. It is little wonder that his publication is self-described as a magazine of speculative poetry. Most of the poetry that appears in the set tends to be prose poetry, a favorite tool of many modern mainstream poets.

While much of the work represents the best poetry in this genre, there is a deadly sense of seriousness and purposefulness that many casual readers may find intimidating and remote. Joron apparently has fallen into the trap that seriousness of purpose is an essential element of the speculative poem.

Additional Anthologies

Following is a list of commercially published anthologies that included poetry. Every year many small-press and fanzine anthologies are published with poetry, but these have a restricted readership base, aiming primarily at hard-core fans or collectors. The anthologies listed below appeal to a broader readership. With each title the poets that are included are noted.

Afterlives, edited by Pamela Sargent. New York: Vintage Books, 1986.
Thomas Disch, Robert Frazier

Again, Dangerous Visions, edited by Harlan Ellison. Garden City, NY: Doubleday & Co., 1972.
Ray Bradbury

Alchemy and Academe, edited by Anne McCaffrey. Garden City, NY: Doubleday & Co, 1970.
L. Sprague de Camp, Virginia Kidd, John Updike

The Altered I, edited by Lee Harding. New York: Berkeley-Windhover, 1978.
Kathryn Buckley and Rob Gerrand

Amazons! edited by Jessica A. Salmonson. New York: DAW Books, 1979.
Emily Brontë, Melanie Kaye

Another Tomorrow, edited by Bernard C. Hollister. New York: Pflaum Pub., 1974.
Louis Salomon, May Swenson

Apeman, Spaceman, Anthropological Science Fiction, edited by
Leon Stover and Harry Harrison. Garden City, NY: Doubleday
& Co., 1968.
Anonymous, Marijane Allen

Bad Moon Rising, edited by Thomas M. Disch. New York: Harper &
Row, 1973.
Marilyn Hacker, Peter Schejeldahl

Basilisk, edited by Ellen Kushner. New York: Ace Books, 1980.
Gordon Grant

Berkley Showcase, Vol. 4, edited by Victoria Schochet and John W.
Silbersack. New York: Berkley, 1981.
Marge Piercy

Berkley Showcase, Vol. 2, edited by Victoria Schochet and John W.
Silbersack. New York: Berkley, 1981.
Thomas M. Disch

The Berserkers, edited by Roger Elwood. New York: Trident Press,
1974.
Virginia Kidd

The Best of Analog, edited by Ben Bova. New York: Baronet
Publishing Co., 1978.
Tim Joseph

Beyond Time, edited by Sandra Ley. New York: Pocket Books, 1976.
Thomas M. Disch

Children of Wonder, edited by William Tenn. New York: Simon &
Schuster, 1953.
Stephen Vincent Benet

Clarion III, edited by Robin Scott Wilson. New York: Signet Books,
1973.
Leonard Isaacs

Computers, Computers, Computers, edited by Dennis L. Van Tassel.
Garden City, NY: Science Fiction Book Club, 1977.
Anonymous

Creations, edited by Isaac Asimov, Martin H. Greenberg, and
George Zebrowski. New York: Crown, 1983.
Traditional Hindu Poem

Dark Forces, edited by Kirby McCaulay. New York: Viking Books,
1980.
Edward Gorey

A Decade of Fantasy and Science Fiction, edited by Robert P. Wells.
Garden City, NY: Doubleday & Co., 1960.
Ogden Nash

Dragons of Darkness, edited by Orson Scott Card. New York: Ace
Books, 1981.
Robert Frazier
Dragons of Light, edited by Orson Scott Card. New York: Ace
Books, 1980.
Steve Rasnic Tem
The Eureka Years, edited by Annette P. McComas. New York:
Bantam Books, 1982.
Anthony Boucher
Fifty Short Science Fiction Tales, edited by Isaac Asimov and Groff
Conklin. New York: Collier Books, 1963.
Poul Anderson
Flying Saucers in Fact and Fiction, edited by Hans S. Santesson.
New York: Lancer Books, 1968.
Nancy Forsythe Coe
The Future at War, edited by Reginald Bretnor. New York: Ace
Books.
Vol. I (1979): Robert Frazier
Vol. II (1980): Robert Frazier
Vol. III (1980): Robert Frazier
Future City, edited by Roger Elwood. New York: Trident Press,
1973.
Thomas M. Disch, Virginia Kidd, S. M. Price
Gosh! Wow! (Sense of Wonder) Science Fiction, no editor given.
New York: Bantam Books, 1982.
Ralph Milne Farley
Greyhaven, edited by Marion Zimmer Bradley. New York: DAW
Books, 1983.
Robert Cook, Diana L. Paxson, Ian Michael Studebaker, Fiona
Lynn Zimmer
Infinity 3, edited by Robert Hoskin. New York: Lancer Books,
1972.
Anthony Wellen
Interfaces, edited by Ursula K. LeGuin and Virginia Kidd. New
York: Ace Books, 1980.
Sonya Dorman, Lawrence Joseph
Invitation to Camelot, edited by Parke Goodwin. New York: Ace
Books, 1988.
Jane Yolen
Lone Star Universe, edited by George Proctor and Steve Utley.
Austin, TX: Heidelberg Publishers, Inc., 1976.
Robert E. Howard

Magazine of Fantasy & Science Fiction: A Thirty Year Retrospective, edited by Edward L. Ferman. Cornwall, CT: Mercury Press, 1979.
John Ciardi, Sonya Dorman, Gerald Jonas, Hilbert Schenck

Mars, We Love You, edited by Jane Hipolito and Willis E. McNelly. Garden City, NY: Doubleday & Co, 1971.
William Fox, Frank Herbert, Irene Jackson

Masterpieces of Terror and the Supernatural, edited by Marvin Kaye. Garden City, NY: Science Fiction Book Club, 1985.
Gottfried August Burger, Ogden Nash

Masters of Darkness, edited by Dennis Etchison. New York: Tor Books, 1986.
Ray Russell

The Nebula Award Stories 17, edited by Joe Haldeman. New York: Holt, Rinehart and Winston, 1985.
Thomas M. Disch, Ken Duffin

Nebula Awards 20, edited by George Zebrowski. New York: Harcourt Brace Jovanovich, 1985.
Helen Ehrlich, Joe W. Haldeman

Nebula Awards 21, edited by George Zebrowski. New York: Harcourt Brace Jovanovich, 1986.
Bruce Boston, Siv Cedering

Nebula Awards 22, edited by George Zebrowski. New York: Harcourt Brace Jovanovich, 1988.
Andrew Joron, Susan Palwick

New Dimensions 8, edited by Robert Silverberg. New York: Harper & Row. 1978.
Peter Dillingham

New Dimensions 9, edited by Robert Silverberg. New York: Harper & Row. 1979.
Peter Dillingham

The New Women of Wonder, edited by Pamela Sargent. New York: Vintage Books, 1978.
Sonya Dorman

New Worlds for Old, edited by Lin Carter. New York: Ballentine Books, 1971.
Clark Ashton Smith, George Sterling

Pawn to Infinity, edited by Fred Saberhagen. New York: Ace Books, 1982.
Robert Frazier

Robots Robots Robots, edited by Harry M. Geduld and Ronald G. Hesman. New York: New York Graphic Society, 1978.
Stephen V. Benet, Louis B. Saloman

Saving Worlds, edited by Roger Elwood and Virginia Kidd. Garden City, NY: Doubleday & Co., 1973.
Thomas M. Disch, D. M. Price

Shot in the Dark, edited by Judith Merrill. New York: Bantam Books, 1950.
Stephen Vincent Benet

A Spadeful of Spacetime, edited by Fred Saberhagen. New York: Ace Books, 1981.
Robert Frazier

The Spawn of Cthulhu, edited by Lin Carter. New York: Ballentine Books, 1971.
Lin Carter, Walter C. DeBill, Jr., Vincent Starrett

Sword and Soceress II, edited by Marion Zimmer Bradley. New York: DAW Books, 1985.
Elizabeth Thompson

2076: The American Tricentennial, edited by Edward Bryant. New York: Pyramid Books, 1977.
Peter Dillingham, Sonya Dorman, Jo Ann Harper, William Jon Watkins

Whispers III, edited by Stuart David Schiff. Garden City, NY: Doubleday & Co., 1981.
Fritz Leiber

Womanspace, edited by Claudia Lampert. Lebanon, NH: New Victoria Publishers, 1981.
Celeste Newbrough

Woman of Wonder, edited by Pamela Sargent. New York: Vintage Books, 1975.
Sonya Dorman

Wondermakers, edited by Robert Hoskins. New York: Fawcett Books, 1972.
Stephen V. Benet

Single-Author Collections

Following is a list of single-author collections of major science fiction, fantasy, and horror writers that contain poetry. However, I have not included single-author collections containing only poetry. While not all the books in this group were commercially published, all had wide distribution.

Poul Anderson. *Homebrew*. Cambridge, MA: NESFA Press, 1976.

Isaac Asimov. *The Far Ends of Time and Earth*. Garden City, NY: Doubleday & Co., 1979.

Isaac Asimov. *Nine Tomorrows*. Garden City, NY: Doubelday & Co., 1959.

Gregory Benford. *In Alien Flesh*. New York: Tor Books, 1986.

Michael Bishop. *Blooded on Arachne*. Sauk City, WI: Arkham House, 1982.

Ray Bradbury. *Dinosaur Tales*. New York: Bantam Books, 1983.

Ray Bradbury. *I Sing the Body Electric*. New York: Alfred A. Knopf, 1969.

John Brunner. *The Book of John Brunner*. New York: DAW Books, 1976.

John Brunner. *From This Day Forward*. Garden City, NY: Doubleday & Co., 1972.

Orson Scott Card. *Unaccompanied Sonata and Other Stories*. New York: Dial Press, 1981.

L. Sprague de Camp. *The Best of L. Sprague de Camp*. Garden City, NY: Science Fiction Book Club, 1978.

L. Sprague de Camp. *Scribblings*. Cambridge, MA: NESFA Press, 1972.

Randall Garrett. *The Best of Randall Garrett*, edited by Robert Silverberg. New York: Pocket Books, 1982.

Randall Garrett. *Take Off!* Virginia Beach, VA: Starblaze Editions, 1980.

Joe W. Haldeman. *Dealing in Futures*. New York: Viking Books, 1985.

Jon Inouye. *A Night Tide*. Culver City, CA: Randen Publishing Co., 1976.

R. A. Lafferty. *Four Stories*. Polk City, IA: Chris Drumm, 1983.

Ursula K. LeGuin. *Always Coming Home*. New York: Harper & Row, 1985.

Walt Liebscher. *Alien Carnival*. North Hollywood, CA: Fantasy House, 1974.

Richard Matheson. *Shock III*. New York: Dell Books, 1966.

Alexei Panshin. *Transmutations*. Elephant, PA: Elephant Books, 1982.

Somtow Sucharitkul. *Fire from the Wine-Dark Sea*. Virginia Beach, VA: Donning, 1983.

J.R.R. Tolkien. *The Lays of Beleriand*. Boston, MA: Houghton Mifflin, 1985.

Chelsea Quinn Yarbo. *Cautionary Tales*. Garden City, NY: Doubleday & Co., 1978.

Jane Yolen. *Dragonfield and Other Stories*. New York: Ace Books, 1985.

Jane Yolen. *Merlin's Booke*. New York: Ace Books, 1986.

III.
Biographical
Directory of Poets

Biographical Directory of Poets

Following is a directory of writers who currently write poetry within the three genres of science fiction, fantasy, and horror. This directory covers only those writers who are active at present, though their work as poets may be sparse at times. For this reason writers such as Hilbert Schenck and Bruce McAllister are not listed. Two of the writers listed, Lin Carter and A. M. Lightner, died during the writing of this book. The directory does include many writers whose poetry and verse are often integrated into larger prose works; however, it is not intended to list every novelist who ever wrote a poem.

After each biographical entry are listed major magazines and key anthologies that have printed the writer's poetry as well as other anthologies and magazines as appropriate. The following abbreviations are used for magazines and anthologies respectively.

MAGAZINES

Amazing — AMZ
Isaac Asimov Science Fiction Magazine — IASFM
Magazine of Fantasy and Science Fiction — F&SF
Owlflight — OF
Pandora — PAN
Scavenger Newsletter — SN
*Star*Line* — SL

ANTHOLOGIES

Aliens and Lovers — A & L
Burning with a Vision — BWV
Holding Your Eight Hands — HYEH
Songs from Unsung Worlds — SFUW

Ackerman, Diane

c/o The Ocean View Press
P.O. Box 4148
Mountain View, CA 94040

Ackerman's career has included a considerable body of poems about science. Her poems are long and use language describing natural phenomena as similes for love and other emotions of the human condition. She writes in first person, an approach that brings an intimacy not often found with the speculative poet.

Anthology Appearances: BWV, *Poly*, SFUM, *The Umbral Anthology of Science Fiction*

Ackerson, Duane

1850 Corina Dr.
Salem, OR 97308

Ackerson has been a leading science fiction poet since 1974. His work predates the emergence of SFPA (Science Fiction Poetry Association). While he had several commercial science fiction anthology appearances, much of his work was for mainstream presses. He edited several poetry anthologies starting in 1970 for the now-defunct Dragonfly Press. Only one, *Rocket Candy*, was predominantly science fiction.

His main influence on the field has been in form. He pioneered prose poetry, one-line poems, and other nontraditional forms in an area that clings to traditional forms while talking about the future. Probably for this reason he has not appeared in the newsstand magazine markets. Some of his prose poetry has been viewed as strictly prose.

The themes of Ackerson's poetry vary greatly, but one strand appears throughout his work: The protagonists are average men and women coping with the vastness of the universe and finding the vastness liberating.

Small-Press Magazine Appearances: *Edge, Magazine of Speculative Poetry,* PAN, SL, *Treaders of Starlight, Velocities*
Anthology Appearances: *Alternities,* BWV, *8th Annual Best SF: 74, Future Pasttimes, Rhysling Anthology 1978, Rhysling Anthology 1979, Sorcerer's Sample Case, The Umbral Anthology of Science Fiction Poetry*
Chapbooks Written by Writer:
The Eggplant & Other Absurdities. Lewiston, ID: Convulence Press, 1978.
UA Flight to Chicago. Lincoln, NE: Best Cellar Press, 1971.
Weathering. Reno, NV: West Coast Poetry Review Press, 1978.
Anthologies Edited by Writer:
Rocket Candy: Speculative Poetry. Salem, OR: Dragonfly Press, 1977.
Awards: Co-winner of Rhysling Award for Short Poem, 1978 and 1979.

Aldiss, Brian

Woodlands, Foxcombe Rd.
Boras Hill
Oxfordshire OX1 5DL
ENGLAND

Brian Aldiss is a prolific poet, but very little of his poetry has appeared in American publications though Holt, Rinehart and Winston did publish a collection of his speculative poems, *Pile: Petals from St. Klaed's Computer.* It would be safe to say that Aldiss's poetry like Aldiss's prose represents the writer's continuing efforts to stretch the definition of science fiction and indeed to determine what constitutes the story or the poem. During the mid-1970s Aldiss coedited the Best SF reprint anthology series with Harry Harrison. Poetry, especially from nongenre sources, found its way on its pages.

Small Press Magazine Appearance: SL
Anthology Appearances: BWV, HYEH
Anthology by Writer: *Pile: Petals from St. Klaed's Computer.* New York: Holt, Rinehart and Winston, 1979.

Allen, Dick

Department of English
University of Bridgeport
Bridgeport, CT 06604

Professor Allen has been deeply involved in science fiction poetry as a writer, critic, and editor. His poetry has always appeared in mainstream publications with one exception, *The Umbral Anthology*. Currently Allen is working on a narrative sonnet sequence of over 200 poems to be called *Space Sonnets*.

Stylistically, there is no typical Allen poem except that his language is always crisp and strong. In choice of themes, he has one overriding concern: He sees poetry as a culturally unifying tool. From his viewpoint, culture has divided into a scientific/technical subculture and a cultural/artistic subculture. Poetry is the tool that enables this writer to view the two separate subcultures as one entity.

Science fiction writers complain that despite their commercial success and the power of their work, their efforts have been ignored by the literary establishment. This has not been Allen's problem. In the past he has received a National Book Critics Circle Award nomination, a National Endowment for the Arts Fellowship, an Ingram Merrill Poetry Writing Fellowship, the Robert Frost Award, and the Union League Award. While none of these honors is specifically for his science fiction work, that work has not hindered his career.

Nevertheless, despite his critical reputation, Allen still has not found a publisher for an anthology of original science fiction poetry that he coedited in the 1970s with Bruce McAllister, a science fiction writer and academic active in poetry at that time.

As an academic Allen has written about science fiction poetry for various learned journals. He is regarded as an authority on teaching science fiction at the college level.

Commercial Magazine Appearance: *The New Yorker*

Small-Press Magazine Appearances: *Agni Review, American Poetry Review, Arts in Society, Cimarron Review, Contemporary Poets of New England, Edge, Kenyon Review, Michigan Quarterly Review, New York Quarterly, Poetry, Poetry Miscellany, Prairie Schooner, Prologue, Western Humanities Review*

Anthology Appearance: *The Umbral Anthology of Science Fiction*

Anderson, Karen

3 Las Palomas
Orinda, CA 94563

Karen Anderson, the wife of Poul Anderson, wrote several heroic fantasy poems for the *Magazine of Fantasy and Science Fiction* in the late 1950s and early 1960s. Thereafter, her poetry fell silent until her collaboration with Poul Anderson on the Ys trilogy developed during the 1980s. The Ys novels, which incorporate the myths described in Frazer's *Golden Bough*, have poetry integrated as chants, prayers, and subtales throughout the work.

Commercial Magazine Appearance: F&SF

Anderson, Poul

3 Las Palomas
Orinda, CA 94563

Poul Anderson wrote several heroic fantasy poems for the *Magazine of Fantasy and Science Fiction* during the 1950s and 1960s. Since then he has frequently used poetry as leitmotifs in many of his fantasy novels, though one, *The Broken Sword* (1953), does predate his F&SF appearances. The poems are in his work because it seems to him that they just fit. Since so many of his novels are adaptions of myths, it is only natural that poems be part of the storytelling. Additionally, Anderson is an enthusiastic singer and several of his songs have become part of the standard repertory of the filksinging subculture of science fiction fandom.

Commercial Magazine Appearances: F&SF, IASFM

Arguelles, Ivan

c/o The Ocean View Press
P. O. Box 4148
Mountain View, CA 94040

Arguelles is a surreal poet whose work has appeared primarily in mainstream poetry publications such as *American Poetry Review* and *Kayak*. However, his work has also been appearing in some small-press publications, especially *Star*Line*, though Arguelles does not view himself as a genre poet. A weakness of surreal poets is that frequently the purpose of their work gets lost in the imagery; however, Arguelles never lets the reader lose sight of what the poem is about.

Small-Press Magazine Appearance: *Velocities*
Anthology Appearance: Poly

Asimov, Isaac

10 W. 66th St., #3-A
New York, NY 10023

It is not surprising that Asimov, the science fiction writer who writes about everything, should have poetry among his countless publications. During the 1950s he wrote several humorous poems that appeared in F&SF and other professional magazines. The poems often celebrated Asimov's numerous "mock disputes" with his colleagues, especially Randall Garrett, himself a very prolific writer of genre poetry. Recently Asimov has written six volumes of limericks, two of them with the distinguished poet John Ciardi. These collections are general in nature, science fiction and fantasy poems being only a small part of the work. However, they are important because Asimov is a major science fiction writer and thus they lend an aura of commercialability to the field.

The limerick collections, however, did have a brief negative impact on the field. The Science Fiction Writers of America (SFWA) is the professional organization for science fiction writers. In order to be a full member of SFWA, a candidate must have a certain number of publications in newsstand magazines or a book. When it was first proposed that poetry publications count toward full membership in SFWA, there was fierce opposition to the idea. Much of the argument centered around the fact that limericks were somehow not appropriate vehicles for achieving full membership, and Asimov's success with limericks was on everyone's mind. However, one can now become a full member of SFWA on poetry publications alone.

Asimov is the editorial director of *Isaac Asimov's Science Fiction Magazine* (IASFM) and the now-defunct *Asimov's Science Fiction Adventure Magazine*. IASFM is one of two major magazines for science fiction poetry.

Commercial Magazine Appearances: *Future Science Fiction, F&SF, IASFM, Science Fiction Quarterly, Science Fiction Stories*

Anthology Appearances:

A Grossary of Limericks (with John Ciardi). New York: Norton, 1981.

Asimov's Sherlockian Limericks. Yonkers, NY: Mysterious Press, 1978.

Lecherous Limericks. New York: Walker, 1975.

Limericks for Children. New York: Caedmon, 1984.

Limericks: Too Gross (with John Ciardi). New York: Norton, 1978.

More Lecherous Limericks. New York: Walker, 1976.

Still More Lecherous Limericks. New York: Walker, 1977.

Athearn, Hope

32 Bretano Way
Greenbrae, CA 94904

A science fiction poet who had earlier established her career in mainstream poetry, Athearn is a popular choice among commercial editors. Her poems are upbeat pieces that reflect the bright, optimistic side of American science fiction. While finely crafted, her poems don't seem to go below the surface images they present.

Commercial Magazine Appearances: AMZ, IASFM
Small-Press Magazine Appearances: SL
Anthology Appearances: *1985 Rhysling Anthology*

Aubrey, Elspeth

P. O. Box 6856
Point Loma, CA 92106

A minor poet in the science fiction genre, Aubrey's work projects an enthusiasm for describing alien landscapes with a passion that equals many fantasy writers' obsession with the land.

Small-Press Magazine Appearance: SL

Ballentine, Lee

c/o The Ocean View Press
P.O. Box 4148
Mountain View, CA 94040

Ballentine has established a career as an able speculative poet. However, his work as a writer of poetry is overshadowed by his importance as a publisher of poetry. Several years ago he established Ocean View Press, a commercial imprint that has published several speculative poetry collections including the complete set of Andrew Joron's *Velocities* magazine.

A new collection of speculative poetry and some prose that he edited, *Poly*, is forthcoming from his publishing house.

Small-Press Magazine Appearance: SL
Anthology Appearances: A&L, *Poly*

Berman, Ruth

2809 Drew Ave., South
Minneapolis, MN 55416

Berman is such a prolific poet and works in so many different areas (mainstream, genre science fiction, religious, fantasy) that it is impossible to describe a typical Berman poem. She has been active in genre work for more than ten years and has had one Rhysling nomination. Yet her name rarely appears in commentaries and discussions of science fiction/fantasy/horror poetry. The problem is that she is foremost a storyteller. This element is often lost when poetry is being discussed. It may also explain why many female genre poets are generally overlooked. Women poets in the field seem to have a stronger grip on narration.

For a time she was a poetry editor of the small-press magazine *Pandora*. Her editorial tastes were wide ranging, and "there were no typical" *Pandora* poets.

Commercial Magazine Appearances: AMZ, IASFM, *Jewish Currents, Reconstructionist Brotherhood, Saturday Review, Toronto Life, Weird Tales*
Small-Press Magazine Appearances: *Beyond, Kansas Quarterly, Poetalk, Poet Lore,* SL, *Tales of the Unanticipated, Texas Quarterly, Tolkien Scrapbook*
Anthology Appearances: AL, BWV, *1987 Rhysling Anthology*

Bessette, George

7 Shamrock Circle
Santa Rosa, CA 95403

A screen writer by trade, Bessette has produced an occasional poem over the years. These are vividly descriptive, which is only appropriate for a screen writer.

Small-Press Magazine Appearance: *Myrddin*

Betancourt, John G.

410 Chester Ave.
Moorestown, NJ 08057

Betancourt's poems have made an occasional appearance in *Amazing*. However, his work as an editor makes Betancourt an important factor in science fiction/fantasy/horror poetry. While still in college, Betancourt founded several small-press science fiction/fantasy magazines, which he later terminated or sold to others. Soon after college, he joined George Scithers's editorial staff at *Isaac Asimov Science Fiction Magazine*. He moved with Scithers to *Amazing*, then left *Amazing* when Scithers did to become part of Scithers's editorial team at the revived *Weird Tales*.

Betancourt thus has been a part of the editorial staff of three major professional publications for science fiction/fantasy/horror poets. The collective decision-making process makes it impossible to say which poem was a Betancourt choice or which poet a Scithers discovery. Scithers, Betancourt, and Darrell Schweitzer (the third member of that group) have been collectively responsible.

Commercial Magazine Appearance: AMZ
Small-Press Magazine Appearances: SL, OF
Anthology Appearance: A&L

Bever, Sue C.

Heath Star Rte.
Lewistown, MT 59457

A poet whose work has focused on hard science fiction with romantic overtones, Bever uses rhyme heavily in her work. Many hard science fiction poets are prejudiced against using rhyme, feeling it trivializes their work; however, in Bever's work, the rhyming emphasizes the emotions she wants to convey. Bever is also active in nongenre poetry.

Small-Press Magazine Appearances: SN, SL

Bishop, Michael

Box 646
Pine Mountain, GA 31822

As a science fiction novelist, Bishop has a well-deserved reputation as one who can integrate extrapolations about the future with commentary on the state of contemporary American society. Between the creation of more than ten novels and numerous short stories he has written an occasional poem, which always has received well-deserved critical attention. His poems are whimsical pieces that talk more about Bishop's own values than traditional science fiction or speculative poem concerns.

Bishop's poem "For the Lady of a Physicist" won the 1979 Rhysling for Long Poem and the 1978 Clark Ashton Smith Award. It dealt with the impact of science upon those not directly involved in it.

Commercial Magazine Appearances: F&SF, IASFM
Small-Press Magazine Appearances: *Shayol*, SL
Anthology Appearances: *Black Hole*, BWV, *1978 Rhysling Anthology, 1979 Rhysling Anthology, 1985 Rhysling Anthology*
Awards: 1979 Rhysling for Long Poem

Bose, Harry

2050 S.W. Runnion Dr.
Pendleton, OR 97801

Bose has specialized in one-line hard science fiction poems. While most poets boast of their ability to use as few words as possible, Bose has made this the core of his work. While there may be controversy over the legitimacy of calling one-line pieces poems, Bose has been able to put emotion and narrative into the handful of words he works with.

Small-Press Magazine Appearances: *Magazine of Speculative Poetry*, SL
Anthology Appearance: BWV

Boston, Bruce

P. O. Box 6398
Albany, CA 94706

Boston is one of the major figures in contemporary science fiction poetry. Like so many of his colleagues, he started his career in the mainstream, then moved into science fiction, fantasy, and horror. Boston makes no bones that his purpose is to entertain the reader, though he would not write a poem for the sole purpose of pleasing readers. His thrust as a poet is as a storyteller. This approach is enhanced by his ability to create tightly constructed paragraphs of description. His poems do not flow. Rather they come out as very tight groups of paragraphs that can stand on their own as poems but are also logical parts of larger works.

Active in building up the infrastructure of science fiction professionals, Boston has served as secretary-treasurer of the Science Fiction Poetry Association and chairman of the Nebula Awards Jury of the Science Fiction Writers of America.

Frequently nominated for the Rhysling, he won it in 1985 in the Short Poem category. He won the 1988 Small Press Writers and Artists Organization Award for Poetry and was their guest of honor at their first annual convention in 1988.

Commercial Magazine Appearances: *Aboriginal SF*, AMZ, IASFM, *Night Cry*

Small-Press Magazine Appearances: *Alpha Adventures, Dreams and Nightmares, Magazine of Speculative Poetry*, PAN, *Portland Review, Scavenger's Newsletter*, SL, *Thumbscrew, Z Miscellaneous*

Anthology Appearances: A&L, BWV, *Lost Lands, Nebula Awards 21, Poly, 1985 Rhysling Anthology*

Anthologies Written by Writer:
The Bruce Boston Omnibus. Mountain View, CA: Ocean View Press, 1987.

Award: 1985 Rhysling for Short Poem

Bradbury, Ray

10265 Cheviot Dr.
Los Angeles, CA 90064

Bradbury is perceived by the average reader as a poet, though his work has rarely appeared in genre publications. The bulk of it is mainstream material, frequently autobiographical. His occasional genre poems are usually odes to the human spirit and technology working together to elevate the human race.

Commercial Magazine Appearances: *Ariel, Galaxy, Galileo, Gamma*, F&SF, *Weird Tales*
Small-Press Magazine Appearance: PN
Anthology Appearances: *Poly, The Umbral Anthology of Science Fiction*
Anthology Written by Writer:
The Complete Poems of Ray Bradbury. New York: Ballentine, 1982.

Brennan, Joseph Payne

26 Fowler St.
New Haven, CT 06515

Brennan is a living link in the history of horror prose and poetry. He was one of the last major writers whose careers were intimately associated with *Weird Tales*. While many writers stayed in the genre when *Weird Tales* first folded in the early 1950s, others drifted away. Some *Weird Tales* poets like Leah Bodine Drake were able to develop second careers at F&SF. Brennan was not among them. His style was always blunt and bloody like the archetypical *Weird Tales* story.

During the 1950s and 1960s he focused on other genres, since there were few markets for the horror writer. Nevertheless, some of his horror poetry and prose occasionally crept into unlikely markets.

During the reemergence of small-press horror magazines, Brennan's horror poetry once again reappeared to a wider audience. Until that time, a self-published horror magazine *Macabre* was the principal outlet for his poetry.

His poems virtually shriek out the emotions that are usually evoked in horror prose and poetry. He does not choose subtlety in his work.

He received the Clark Ashton Smith Award for Life Achievement in 1978 and the World Fantasy Award for Life Achievement in 1982.

Commercial Magazine Appearances: *Commonweal, Twilight Zone, Weird Tales*
Small-Press Magazine Appearances: *Beyond the Fields We Know, Borderland, Cross Plains, Fantasy Crossroads, Literary Magazine of Fantasy and Terror, Macabre, Night Voyages,*

Omniumgathum, Orange Street Journal, Voices, Weird Book, Whispers

Anthologies Written by the Writer:

As Evening Advances. New Haven, CT: Macabre House, 1978.

Edges of Night. New Haven, CT: Macabre House, 1974.

Nightmare Need. New Haven, CT: Macabre House, 1964.

Webs of Time. New Haven, CT: Macabre House, 1979.

Bretnor, Reginald

Box 1481

Medford, OR 97501

A State Department official turned free-lance writer, Bretnor has been active in genre science fiction for over four decades. Much of his creative output has been devoted to two series of extremely funny, if overdone, stories, "Through Space and Time with Ferdinand Feghoot" (Feghoot being a Dr. Who–type character whose wanderings in Time and Space cause all Feghoot tales to resound with horrendous puns) and the "Schimmelhorn" stories (Schimmelhorn being an incoherent Pennsylvania Dutch genius whose inventions inexplicably work).

His output as a poet within the science fiction genre has been very small but is written with the same broad humor as his stories. The only notable aspect of his work as a poet was that one of his Ferdinand Feghoot tales was written as a Haiku.

His importance to science fiction poetry was as an editor. He edited a three-volume anthology of military science fiction, *The Future at War* (New York: Ace, 1979–80). For each of the three volumes he had a poem by Robert Frazier, an early major commercial appearance by this major science fiction poet.

Military science fiction is the hardest of hard science fiction, a subgenre where extrapolations in technology and scientific theory are crucial to the plot of the story. Hard science fiction is the basic core of modern American science fiction. Its aficionados, if not its writers, have been resistant to poetry as a legitimate form for hard science fiction writers.

The appearance of Frazier's poems in a hard science fiction anthology represents a significant breakthrough for science fiction poetry.

Commercial Magazine Appearances: AMZ, F&SF

Brunner, John

c/o Carnell Literary Agency
Rowenbury Bungalow
Sawbridgeworth
Essex CM20 2EX
ENGLAND

Brunner, like Aldiss, has written a considerable body of science fiction and speculative poetry. Yet, very little of it has appeared in this country. Like much of his prose, Brunner's poetry is concerned with individuals attempting to function in a society that is indifferent to their individuality.

Anthology Appearance: HYEH

Bryant, Ed

c/o Jelm Mountain Publications
209 Park
Laramie, WY 82070

Bryant's best work is short stories with a bleak, depressing outlook. His occasional poems are light pieces that seem more concerned with artfully playing with words than any larger purpose.

Commercial Magazine Appearance: F&SF
Anthology Appearances: BWV, *1979 Rhysling Anthology*

Buburuz, Cathy

2419 Klein Place
Regina, Saskatchewan
CANADA S4U 1M4

Buburuz's work focuses on the impact of childhood terrors on one's life. The supernatural elements in her poetry seem almost superfluous to the terror that she describes.

Small-Press Magazine Appearances: *Pantophobia, Prisoners of Night*, SN, *Terror Time Again*

Bunch, David

P. O. Box 12233
Soulard Station
St. Louis, MO 63157

David Bunch is not an easy writer to describe. Both his prose and poetry seem to follow rules that are peculiar to Bunch. Frequently his characters speak to the reader in a cadence that seems appropriate for a robot in a low-budget science fiction thriller. Yet, he does captivate the reader with his dark satirical dystopian pieces. Despite the oddity of his language, Bunch's work is approachable for the reader. It just takes some getting used to.

Commercial Magazine Appearances: AMZ, IASFM, F&SF
Small-Press Magazine Appearance: SL
Anthology Appearances: BWV, *Poly*

Burkhardt, Sandra Stuart

7 Gales Point
Manchester, MA 01944

Burkhardt is best known as a romantic science fiction poet. Her work leans toward interspecies amour. While her work does contain a fair amount of physical description, it does not come off as burlesques about bestiality. Rather, her pieces insist that love is the mark of civilized beings no matter their external form.

Small-Press Magazine Appearances: OF, SL
Anthology Appearance: A&L

Burwasser, Lee

1516 U Street, NW
Washington, DC 20009

Burwasser's career is typical of so many writers who focus their talents on writing filksong verses for commercial markets such as Off-Centaur. While a college student she became active in the science fiction fannish community by first attending Star Trek conventions. At Star Trek and general science fiction conventions she became exposed to filksinging. Burwasser became a filk writer in her own right. She was a cofounder of *Apa-Filk.*

In the science fiction community an Apa is a group of fanzine publisher/editors who exchange their publications among each other, as well as selling to subscribers. Apas tend to be specialized, topic-oriented groups (media, art, fiction).

In *Apa-Filk* her publication was *Strum Und Drang.* Obviously, extremely bad puns are an important part of the science fiction fannish community.

Burwasser also cofounded *Worksmithy,* an Apa devoted to poetry. There her publication was *Thulur.* In 1987, after twenty years, she started to sell her material to a professional publisher, in this case Off-Centaur. Off-Centaur has now been liquidated.

Like so many filk writers her work is based heavily in the romance of space flight and science fiction films, especially "Star Trek."

Butler, Jack

5820 Hawthorne
Little Rock, AK 72207

The work and career of Jack Butler is proof that science fiction poetry is clearly an integrated part of American poetry. Apart from appearances in *Star*Line,* most of Butler's genre work has been published in major mainstream publications such as *Atlantic, The New Yorker,* and *Little Review.* Certainly not all of Butler's work is science fiction–oriented. His appearances prove that major mainstream publications are open to genre poetry.

As a poet Butler is certainly powerful. In his work he speaks directly to the reader with crisp, precise language that demands attention. Butler is always attempting to reconcile the universe that can be quantified by data and the universe that can only be proven by belief.

Ironically his stature within the science fiction genre is relatively obscure because most of his genre work has appeared in mainstream publications. Thus many science fiction poetry fans are not familiar with his work. It is a curious reversal of the old problem that when science fiction was a literary ghetto, many of its better writers were unknown to readers and critics outside the field.

Commercial Magazine Appearances: *Atlantic, Cavalier, The New Yorker*

Small-Press Magazine Appearances: *Little Review, Nebo, New Orleans Review, Poetry Northwest*, SL
Anthology Written by Writer:
The Kid Who Wanted to be a Spaceman. Little Rock, AK: August House, 1986.

Calder, David

38 Canning St.
Liverpool L8 7NP
ENGLAND

Calder is a major English poet. Science fiction is merely one of several themes that he deals with in his work. Many of his non–science fiction poems also deal with themes that the science fiction poet uses such as human alienation from technology.

His particularly science fiction poems focus on space exploration. He is a poet who does tell a story in his work, especially in his science fiction poems. His protagonists find that the exploration of the universe is a reflection of their own explorations into their own identity and purpose of life. However, Calder does not fall into the trap of having his characters speak only to themselves. There is communication between the reader and Calder.

He was a 1980 Rhysling nominee for Long Poem.

Anthology Appearances: BWV, *1980 Rhysling Anthology, The Umbral Anthology of Science Fiction Poetry*
Chapbook Written by Writer:
Spaced. Liverpool, England: Toulouse Press, 1979.

Carter, Lin

Box 501
Montclair, NJ 07042

Either you love Lin Carter's work or you hate Lin Carter's work. There seems to be no room for neutrality.

Carter has been an endless producer of potboiler fantasy novels for almost thirty years. To some his work typifies all the worst features of genre fiction, that is, stereotypical characters, minimal plots, and needlessly baroque language. To his admirers his work represents pure entertainment without pretentiousness but with tongue firmly in cheek.

His poetry has the same qualities (or faults, depending on your point of view) as his prose. Most of his poetry has been used in his novels, primarily to give his characters something to quote when words otherwise fail them. However, some of his poetry has appeared in various modern reincarnations of *Weird Tales* as well as an Arkham House collection of his poems based largely on the Lovecraft canon.

Commercial Magazine Appearance: *Weird Tales*
Anthology Written by Writer:
    Dreams from R'Lyeh. Sauk City, WI: Arkham House, 1975.

Choo, Mary E.

5711 Wallace Rd.
Richmond, BC
CANADA V7E 2C4

A new poet, Choo's work seems oriented to explaining genre themes to readers who are not necessarily science fiction/fantasy/ horror fans.

Small-Press Magazine Appearances: *Cross-Canada Writer's Quarterly, Scrivener,* SL

Christopher, Joe R.

Department of English and Languages
School of Arts and Sciences
Tarleton State University
Stephenville, TX 76402

Christopher, an English professor at Tarleton State University in Texas, is an anomaly in the science fiction/fantasy/horror poetry field. In mainstream poetry, poets may acquire a critical reputation and following by appearing in important but nonpaying publications such as academic journals. In science fiction/fantasy/horror poetry, the reverse is true. A poet's appearance in paying publications (either newsstand or small press) is the key to a poet's influence in the field.

However, Christopher has never appeared in a paying publication as a poet. All his appearances to date have either been in academic journals or in fanzines, those ubiquitous amateur publications that play important roles in the discussion of ideas within the three genres as well as a training ground for new prose and poetry writers.

His poetry can be divided into categories. One is humorous light verse (frequently limericks) that find a niche in major fanzines such as *Niekas*. The other category are serious poems, pieces that are either homages to major fantasy writers or pastiches of their style. These find a home in academic journals such as *Mythlore* and the *Charles Williams Newsletter*.

Recently his attention has been focused on long narrative poems (1,000 lines or so) that are intended to be symbolic pieces with a hint of fantasy. Probably when they are complete, they will be self-published chap books.

Christopher maintains two disparate traditions. One is that of the pure amateur fanzine writer who writes for the pleasure of writing and the love of science fiction/fantasy/horror. The other is the serious scholar for whom poetry is a part of his work in the scholarly tradition.

Small-Press Magazine Appearances: *Charles Williams Newsletter, Mythlore, Niekas, Outworlds, Rampant Guinea Pig*

Cohen, Mitchell

2615 Homecrest Ave.
Brooklyn, NY 11235

Cohen has a knack for folding whimsey into poems of science. The results are poems that are light verse but not frivolous. In his work, Cohen seems to be looking at the universe in a simple way in an effort to reduce it to a manageable scale.

Small-Press Magazine Appearance: SL

Colander, Valerie Nieman

P. O. Box 1614
Fairmont, WV 26554

Colander's work is interesting in that the genre elements in her science fiction and fantasy poems are so understated and subtle as to be overlooked. At first blush it would seem that the only thing that qualifies her work as science fiction or fantasy is that it appears in a science fiction or fantasy magazine. Yet, when the reader does notice the genre element in the work, then the poem acquires that distinction, which makes it a genre poem. A mainstream poet as well, Colander has started work on a science fiction novel.

Small-Press Magazine Appearances: *Magazine of Speculative Poetry, Proof Rock, Space & Time,* SL, *White Rock Review*

Collings, Michael R.

1089 Sheffield Place
Thousand Oaks, CA 91360

While Collins has generated a considerable body of science fiction/fantasy/horror poetry, he is equally important as a critic and reviewer of genre poetry. Science fiction/fantasy/horror poetry is not the only area that attracts Collins as a critic and a commentator, but it constitutes a large part of his work. As a commentator, he seems most interested in defining the role and importance of poetry within the body of science fiction literature.

He views his critical work as a bridge between the science fiction fannish community and the academic literary community. In a sense he is a translator who attempts to explain the viewpoints of two disparate and sometimes mutually contemptuous communities to each other.

However, Collins the poet is as important as Collins the critic. Like many genre poets, Collins integrates traditional form such as the sonnet with science fiction, fantasy, or horror themes. Frequently his language has an archaic flavor that clashes with futuristic themes. The result is that the reader is made aware that the future is not some distinct entity that is independent of the past and present. Future, past, and present are all of the same cloth.

There has been considerable attention paid to his work which has resulted in several Rhysling, SPWAO, and even Nebula nominations. His poems were nominated in the short story category of the Nebulas. He is currently a member of the faculty of Pepperdine University and poetry editor for *Dialogue: A Journal of Mormon Thought.*

Commercial Magazine Appearance: *Fantasy Book*
Small-Press Magazine Appearances: *Footsteps of Space & Time,* SL, *Velocities*
Anthology Appearances: A&L, *1981 Rhysling Chapbook, 1982 Rhysling Chapbook, 1986 Rhysling Chapbook*

Chapbook Written by Writer:
Naked to the Sun: Dark Visions of Apocalypse. Mercer Island, WA: Starmount House, 1985.

Compton, S. R.

2907 M. L. King Jr. Way, Apt. A
Berkeley, CA 94703

Compton did not consciously set out to be a science fiction poet, though he has always been a science fiction fan and reader. As a poet, he uses romantic and pastoral images to comment upon the technical artifacts of Western civilization and the civilization that produces such objects. Science fiction markets are attracted to this type of poetry. As a result, earlier sales to these markets have encouraged him to keep writing science fiction. He has received critical notice for his work as well as a Rhysling nomination in 1987 for Short Poem.

Small-Press Magazine Appearances: SL, *Velocities*
Anthology Appearances: A&L, BWV, *1987 Rhysling Anthology*

Cording, H. J.

R. D. 2
Kaitaia, New Zealand

Cording is a New Zealand horror writer whose publications have been primarily in the small press in this country and Canada. He is one of the few genre poets who is not a storyteller. His poems have been based on ideas that do not fit readily into the context of prose stories. Highly regarded in small-press circles, he was nominated for the SPWAO poetry award in 1985.

Small-Press Magazine Appearances: *Maplecade, 2 A.M.*

Crawford, Dan

940 N. Franklin
Manchester, IA 52057

Crawford is a writer who sees his poems as primarily pieces to amuse and entertain. If they edify, then that is well and good. His pieces tend to sound like excerpts from amusing folksongs. This is not surprising. Crawford is a frequent writer of filksongs, folksongs with new verses based on science fiction, fantasy, or horror fiction. Filksinging is a major after-hours fannish activity at most science fiction and fantasy conventions.

Commercial Magazine Appearance: AMZ
Small-Press Magazine Appearances: *Beyond, Doppleganger, Infinitium,* SN

Crawford, Gary W.

P. O. Box 80051
Baton Rouge, LA 70898-0051

Crawford has written very few horror poems. His importance in genre poetry has been as editor. He edits *Gothic,* a scholarly journal that focuses on the gothic elements of supernatural literature including poetry.

Recently he founded *Supernatural Poetry,* a literary magazine devoted to the subject of its title. Crawford may be a traditionalist in his approach to poetry, but as an editor, he is open to all forms of well-crafted poems of fantasy and horror. Major poets such as Janet Fox, Joey Froehlich, and Denise Dumars have appeared in its pages.

Small-Press Magazine Appearances: *Dreams & Nightmares, Grue,* SL

Crouch, Annette S.

P. O. Box 55125
Stockton, CA 95205-8625

A horror poet, Crouch's poems are atypical for the genre. Her work tends to be humorous and with upbeat endings. Currently she is a columnist for *The Nightmare Express,* a market newsletter for horror writers. She has put together *The Bear Essential,* an anthology of short stories and poems about bears, which has not yet found a publisher. As it happens so often with small-press publications, she sold poems to magazines that promptly fold after they buy the poem.

Commercial Magazine Appearance: *Hoofstrikes*
Small-Press Magazine Appearances: *The Nightmare Express, Potboiler, Supernatural Poetry*

Dale, Jo Anna

704 Ponca Dr.
Independence, MO 64056

A retired federal employee, Dale's work has focused on short humorous pieces with science fiction and fantasy themes. Much of her work as a mainstream poet has appeared in markets that cater to rural families such as *Capper's*.

Small-Press Magazine Appearances: *Beyond, Scavenger's Newsletter*

Daniels, Keith Allen

1015-19 N. W. 21st Ave.
Gainesville, FL 32609

The expression of the idea in a poem is as important to Daniels as is the idea itself. His language resonates within the reader. Yet, Daniels's poems have a characteristic that many see as a flaw. They frequently seem remote and detached. The results are admirable pieces that seem to have little or no emotional bond with the reader. This is ironic because science fiction/fantasy/horror poets frequently decry this problem in mainstream poetry. While Daniels works in all three genres, the coldness that often prevails in his poems conveys a sense of horror. Probably the coldness in his work has closed off newsstand outlets to him despite the fact that he has worked as a genre poet for over twelve years.

Daniels started appearing when the small-press segment of science fiction/fantasy/horror publications developed in the early 1970s. He seems to be the best example of the theory that the modern rise of science fiction/fantasy/horror poetry is largely due to the creation of small-press genre publications.

However, being in the small-press ghetto has not prevented Daniels from receiving the attention that his work demands. He has received nominations both for the Rhysling and the Clark Ashton Smith awards.

Small-Press Magazine Appearances: *Beyond, Catalyst, Dreams & Nightmares, Fungi, Grue, The Muse Newsletter, Pandora*, SN, SL, 2 *A.M.*

Chapbooks Written by Writer:
The Gryphon. Gainesville, FL: Self-published, 1987.
Weird Sonnets. Gainesville, FL: Self-published, 1981.
Anthology Appearance: *1987 Rhysling Anthology*

Dann, Jack

71 Mill St.
Binghamton, NY 13903

Well known for his short stories that focus on individuals' conflict with stratified societies, Dann has produced poems that the individual sees in a different life. His poetry explores the feeling of those who are intent on prioritizing their individualness (no matter the cost) in a universe of splendor and vast scale.

Small-Press Magazine Appearance: SL
Anthology Appearance: BWV

Darlington, Andrew

c/o Ocean View Books
P. O. Box 4148
Mountain View, CA 94040

Darlington is one of the few English poets who appear with any frequency in American genre publications. Many of his poems deal with the clichés that are found in science fiction. However, his work looks at the reasoning for those clichés, their essential core of truth.

There is a downside to this upbeat look. Frequently the narrative voice of his poems expresses disbelief at the vastness of the universe. There seems to be an implicit desire for a smaller, more human-dimensioned place.

He is the publisher/editor of the British small-press magazine *Ludd's Mills*.

Anthology Appearances: *Poly, 1986 Rhysling Anthology, 1987 Rhysling Anthology, The Umbral Anthology of Science Fiction Poetry*

DeLint, Charles

P. O. Box 9480
Ottawa, Ontario
CANADA K1G 3V2

DeLint is a fantasy writer who started in poetry but who now does high-fantasy novels, frequently set in modern urban settings. In both his prose and his poetry, he explores what he calls the Mystery. His work looks at the spiritual component of things, that for which their physical form is shadow.

A prolific writer, DeLint writes for three different science fiction/fantasy trade magazines, *Short Form, Horrorstruck,* and *Other Realms.* DeLint also has an imprint, Triskell Press, which formerly published two fantasy magazines that were showcases for poetry, *Beyond the Fields We Know* and *Dragonbane.* Occasionally he has written under the pseudonym Wendelessen.

Small-Press Magazine Appearances: *Amanita Brandy, Dark Fantasy, Simba, Weirdbook*
Anthology Appearance: A&L

Devin, John

125 Spencer Rd.
Devon, PA 19333

John Devin is a pseudonym of playwright John Sevcik. In the last several years Devin has written many poems for *Isaac Asimov's* and *Amazing.* His attraction to the three genres is their ability to reinfuse traditional themes with new vitality and a new outlook.

During the early 1980s he served as an assistant editor under George Scithers at both *Isaac Asimov's* and *Amazing.* Perhaps it was this editorial apprenticeship that led him to use traditional meters and stanzas in his work. Scithers always had an editorial preference for traditional forms.

Additionally his poems are stories rather than some reflection, humorous or tragic, on some science fiction cliché. His poems seem to be the clearest examples of the Elgin definition for a science fiction poem, a narrative component and a science component.

Despite his obvious skill, his poems frequently seem like good textbook examples of science fiction poems rather than pieces that represent an artist's true feelings. Perhaps this is why he has never been nominated for a Rhysling.

Commercial Magazine Appearances: AMZ, IASFM

Dickson, Gordon

c/o Kirby McCauley Ltd.
425 Park Ave., South
New York, NY 10016

Dickson is probably the best military science fiction novelist in the genre. His novels view professional soldiers as the only honest men and women in a civilization dominated by corrupt politicians and indifferent civilians. This theme is not uncommon in science fiction.

In many of his military novels, the ballads, poems, and songs of the military subculture appear. His work as a poet has been limited to heroic ballads for F&SF plus some filksongs based on his novels for an Off-Centaur album devoted to the Dorsai (a military subculture that play a major role in his novels) called *Songs of the Dorsai* (cat. #83090).

Dickson is a filksinger, and probably his original songs find their way into the repertoire of the filksingers.

Commercial Magazine Appearance: F&SF

Digby, Thomas G.

1800 Rice St.
Los Angeles, CA 90042

Tom Digby has rapidly acquired a reputation as a very fine romantic poet who can blend romance with traditional science fiction elements into fine professional work. His nomination for the 1988 Rhysling for long poetry is clear indication that romance is still considered an important element among science fiction poets.

Small-Press Magazine Appearances: SL, *Tales of the Unanticipated*

Dillingham, Peter

c/o Ocean View Press
P. O. Box 4148
Mountain View, CA 94040

Dillingham has been active as a science fiction poet since the early 1970s when original anthologies became a major segment of the science fiction market. Readers may be familiar with his work that has appeared in the various Pournelle anthologies, which are frequently reprinted. His language is terse and choppy. Indeed, each line of his poems is a self-contained, vivid piece of description.

Most of his work is concerned with the vast natural forces at play in the universe. Yet, in these poems, the human element may be dwarfed but never overwhelmed by those forces. He was publisher/editor of *Cthulu Calls*, a Lovecraft-oriented small-press magazine.

Small-Press Magazine Appearance: SL
Anthology Appearances: *Black Holes, Endless Frontiers* (Vols. I & II), *Poly, There Will Be War* (Vols. III & IV), *1978 Rhysling Anthology, 1981 Rhysling Anthology*

Disch, Tom

Marie Rodell-Frances Collin Agency
110 W. 40th St.
New York, NY 10018

Disch is the prototype of the new science fiction writer. His career started in mainstream literary journals as both a prose writer and poet, though it really started in mainstream small press during the 1950s. Disch has been an angry voice that frequently blasted the science fiction genre for smugness and willingness to be ordinary.

Almost from the beginning of his science fiction career his poetry was published. Starting with the "New Wave" incarnation of *New Worlds*, Disch's poetry has focused on the clichés of science fiction and has savaged it repeatedly. He has an anger about the shortcomings of the science fiction genre, and poetry has been his medium to display it. While most serious science fiction poets favor optimistic or at least upbeat approaches, Disch still forces his peers and the reader to look at the downside of American science fiction. Such is his skill and voice as a poet that the newsstand magazines buy his poetry, even though editorial policies generally favor upbeat material.

In 1981, his poem "On Science Fiction" won the Rhysling for Long Poem.

Commercial Magazine Appearances: AMZ, F&SF
Small-Press Magazine Appearances: PAN, SL
Anthology Appearances: BWV, HYEH, *Poly, 1981 Rhysling Anthology*
Award: 1981 Rhysling for Long Poem

Donaldson, Jr., C. Clark

3450 N. W. 171 Terrace
Miami, FL 33056

A poet who has occasionally forayed into science fiction, Clark's genre work has focused on expanding the possibilities of lyric poetry.

Small-Press Magazine Appearances: *Futurific*, SL

Dorman, Sonya

c/o The Virginia Kidd Agency
Box 278
Milford, PA 18337

Dorman is the forerunner of a particular class of American science fiction poets who started their careers as mainstream poets and drifted into science fiction because those markets wanted to buy their output.

From the early 1960s until the early 1970s almost all her output of science fiction poetry was for the *Magazine of Fantasy and Science Fiction*. At the same time she started a short-story career in science fiction, again mostly for F&SF and the original anthologies that proliferated during the 1960s and 1970s. Ironically she sold only one poem to an original anthology, *2076*.

Her poetry, whether genre or not, seems dominated by a sense of autumn. Her work frequently describes locales that are going through a time of slow, gentle decay. Stylistically, she understates what needs to be said in her work. She does not use flamboyant language or elaborate poetic structures. In the last several years she has gone back to writing only poetry. Her output is now primarily for chapbooks and mainstream journals.

Commercial Magazine Appearances: F&SF, *Quark*
Anthology Appearances: BWV, *1978 Rhysling Anthology, 1983*
    Rhysling Anthology, The Umbral Anthology of Science Fiction
    Poetry
Chapbooks Written by Writer:
    The Far Traveler. La Crosse, WI: Juniper Press, 1980.
    Palace of Earth. Orono, ME: Puckerbrush Press, 1984.
    A Paper Raincoat. Orono, ME: Puckerbrush Press, 1976.
    Poems. Columbus, OH: Ohio State University Press, 1970.
    Stretching Fence. Athens, OH: Ohio University Press, 1975.
Award: Co-winner, 1978 Rhysling Short Poem

Dorr, James S.

1404 E. Atwater
Bloomington, IN 47401

A full-time free-lance writer in fiction and nonfiction, Dorr uses his poetry to entertain the reader, demonstrating alternate viewpoints on various science fiction and fantasy topics. In most cases there is no clear distinction as to when he is writing in the science fiction or the fantasy mode. Dorr prefers to use traditional forms as a poet. To him such constraint is a discipline that helps improve his prose style as well as a general ability to use words.

Commercial Magazine Appearances: *Aboriginal SF, Fantasy Book*
Small-Press Magazine Appearance: SL
Anthology Appearance: *1987 Rhysling Anthology*

Dragwyla, Yael

P. O. Box 45792
Seattle, WA 98145-0792

Dragwyla is probably the only English-language poet who can trace her ancestry to Vlad Tepes, the Transylvania count who served as the model for Count Dracula. It is probably not surprising that Dragwyla is a practicing magician and that much of her output as a poet is concerned with the various disciplines. With a hard science background in college, her poems frequently explore the possibilities of a syncretic relationship between the sciences and magic.

Few poets in the genre actually write about the nature of magic in the same way that poets write about scientific phenomena. This may be surprising, since magic is a basic component of fantasy in the same way that science is a basic component of science fiction. The probable reason is that few writers actually believe that magic is more than folklore, that it does exist. Dragwyla, being a professional magician in the hermetic sense, obviously believes in the existence of magic. Her poetry has appeared only in publications concerned with magic. She is the publisher/editor of *BV1-Pacifica Newsletter,* an eclectic publication.

Small-Press Magazine Appearances: *The Cincinnati Journal of Ceremonial Magick, Popular Reality, Seditious Delicious*

Dumars, Denise

11843 Eucalyptus Ave., #D
Hawthorne, CA 90250

Creepiness seems to be the heart of a Dumars poem. Though she works in all three genres as well as poems outside science fiction/fantasy/horror, her poems set in the horror genre stand out from the others.

Horror poems tend to be morbid and overwritten. While her poems can be described as morbid, she uses sparse language. The result is a true sense of horror in her work rather than a burlesque laden with clichés. In 1986 she won the SPWAO Award for Poetry. Currently she is a columnist for *The Writer.*

Small-Press Magazine Appearances: *Beyond, Dreams & Nightmares, Grue, Pulpsmith,* SN, SL, *Thumbscrew*
Chapbook Written by Writer:
   Sheet Lightning. Hawthorne, CA: Terata Publications, 1987.
Award: 1986 SPWAO Award for Poetry

Dunn, Patricia C.

5985 Yukon St., #5
Arvada, CO 80004

Dunn's work in science fiction and fantasy poetry has one common element, a sense of vastness of the universe but that man has a purpose in it. While this theme is not uncommon for genre poets, it dominates

Dunn's work. It is not surprising that Walt Whitman is as important an influence on Dunn's work as any genre poet.

Small-Press Magazine Appearances: *Shadows Of*, SL

Dutcher, Roger

> 1537 Washburn
> Beloit, WI 53511

A poet who has been active in science fiction since 1977, Dutcher can evoke emotions in his genre work. Many science fiction poets attempt to infuse their work with the quality of emotion but fail because the emotional component seems superimposed on the poem. Dutcher seems to be able to describe the emotion and work his way out into the larger poem.

From 1979 to 1985 he was the publisher-editor of *Uranus,* a science fiction poetry magazine. In 1984 he cofounded with Mark Rich (and now serves as coeditor) the *Magazine of Speculative Poetry.* Curiously while he has been very successful in commercial publications, he has not been visible in many small-press genre markets.

Commercial Magazine Appearance: AMZ
Small-Press Magazine Appearances: *Magazine of Speculative Poetry,* SN, SL
Anthology Appearances: A&L, BWV

Effinger, George Alec

> Box 15183
> New Orleans, LA 70175

While primarily a science fiction novelist and short-story writer, Effinger has started writing poetry. He has used poetry in his longer prose works. The poetry, usually outrageously bad, is written by the novels' characters as a way to describe themselves. His few free-standing poems are also descriptions of characters.

Commercial Magazine Appearance: F&SF

Egan, Thomas M.

6936 43rd Ave.
Woodside, NY 11377

Egan, a poet whose best work is in horror, can be described as a writer in the Twilight Zone mode. In his poems he creates experiences that are outside the normal human experience. At the same time his poems skillfully link those outer experiences to our own real-world experiences. The result is subtle poems that are reminiscent of "Twilight Zone" episodes but without the 1950s political liberalism that seemed to be shoveled into every plot. Though Egan has been active for almost a decade, he has not received the attention that his work deserves because his work is so understated.

Small-Press Magazine Appearances: *Apogee, Approaches, Beyond the Fields We Know, Dark Fantasy, Dragonfields, Eldritch Tales, Fantasy Crosswinds, Mythlore, Mythellany, Nyctalops, Simba*

Elgin, Suzette Haden

Rt. 4, Box 192-E
Huntsville, AK 72740

Elgin has worked both as a professional writer and as a scholar in the field of linguistics. Her poetry, a minor part of her output as a science fiction writer, does not fit smoothly into any one form or theme. However, her pieces tend to be merry works of verse that are frequently set to music. However, her importance to science fiction poetry lies in the fact that, in 1977, she founded the Science Fiction Poetry Association, an organization that has played a seminal role in the reintroduction of poetry into the major science fiction magazine markets as well as serving as a forum for genre poets to meet and interact with each other. Despite its name, the Science Fiction Poetry Association is concerned with all three genres (science fiction, fantasy, and horror).

Elgin is also noted for her one law on the definition of what is a science fiction poem. Elgin's law simply states that a science fiction poem must have a narrative component and a science component. This definition has become a widely used but by no means universally accepted definition for science fiction poetry. It is also an ongoing source of argument among poets as to its accuracy.

Many of her science fiction novels are based on the Ozark hill culture of her native Missouri. Chants, folksongs, magic incantations, and folk tales play an important part in these novels, known as the "Ozark Trilogy," and its sequels.

Commercial Magazine Appearances: AMZ, IASFM
Small-Press Magazine Appearance: SL
Anthology Appearances: BWV, *1987 Rhysling Anthology*

Eng, Stephen

P. O. Box 60072
Nashville, TN 37206

Eng is better known as a scholar in the field of gothic literature than as a poet. He has produced many fine poems of the supernatural.

His poems are always tightly constructed in traditional forms. He is probably the only active poet who works in the true gothic tradition, though he does write poems in other genres. For example, his poem "Story Books and Treasure Maps," which co-won the 1979 Rhysling for Short Poem, was an homage to the swashbuckling tradition in popular literature.

He serves as assistant editor of the scholarly journal, *The Romantacist*.

Commercial Magazine Appearance: AMZ
Small-Press Magazine Appearances: OF, PAN, SL
Anthology Appearances: A&L, *1981 Rhysling Anthology, 1986 Rhysling Anthology*

Forest, Jody

P. O. Box 666
Summerland, CA 93067

A surreal writer whose prose work has appeared in surreal and underground publications, Forest's poems are an unusual mixture of surreal and Lovecraftian elements. The poems cannot be described any other way.

He has also used poetry in his prose work to give the texture that you would associate with Tolkien. Forest is presently working on an Atlantis myth novel that is using a large number of poems for the same effect.

Commercial Magazine Appearance: *Santa Barbara News & Review*
Small-Press Magazine Appearances: *Mudborn Press, Salvador Dali Fan Club News, Terror Time Again*

Fox, Janet

519 Ellinwood
Osage City, KS 66523

Fox is one of the new generation of science fiction, fantasy, and horror writers who seems comfortable in either prose or poetry. She is a voluminous writer, and most of her sales, especially her poetry, have been in small-press magazines.

It is hard to imagine why she has not penetrated more fully the newsstand commercial markets. Her poetry usually has both the formal structure and the humorous twist that the commercial editors generally favor. Her work can best be described as the written equivalent of a Charles Addams cartoon: black, painful, and funny.

She is also well known as the publisher/editor of *Scavenger's Newsletter*, a newsletter on science fiction/fantasy/horror markets and a market in its own right for poetry.

Commercial Magazine Appearances: *Fantasy Review, Weird Tales*
Small-Press Magazine Appearances: *Aquila, Bloodrake, Bleeding Virgin, Dreams & Nightmares, Fungi, Magazine of Speculative Poetry, Moonscape, SL, Z Miscellaneous*
Anthology Appearances: *A Walk in the Dark,* BWV, *Star/Sword Poetry Chapbook I,* A&L

Frazier, Robert

Box 1370
Nantucket, MA 02554

Every literary field has dominant writers, persons whose work defines standards by which others are judged. The three genres of science fiction, fantasy, and horror have been particularly influenced by key individuals. In science fiction, fantasy, and horror poetry Robert Frazier has performed this role.

It's difficult to assess Frazier's work because he is so prolific that it seems that every other poem in print is his. The key to his popularity is twofold. He is probably the best craftsman working in the field.

Frazier knows the tools and the language of poetry. Second, there is always a commanding, overriding passion that dominates his poetry. In a Frazier poem, there is no such thing as an objective narrator. No matter whether the poem is speculative, science, traditional science fiction, high fantasy, or horror, that passion marches through the work.

Frazier was not a genre poet until he read Lucie-Smith's *Holding Your Eight Hands*. The anthology demonstrated to him the possibilities of the fantastic for poetry. However, when he first started to work in the genre, he focused his attention on poems of science rather than science fiction poems. Later his work turned to more traditional science fiction, fantasy, or horror themes depending on the market. Yet even in his speculative poems of science, there is such a strong passion.

During much of the Science Fiction Poetry Association life, Frazier edited its publication *Star*Line*. He continued the tradition of its first editor, Suzette Elgin, and made the publication a brilliant showcase of poems in all genres as well as a fiery forum for debate among poets. Previously he published and edited *The Anthology of Speculative Poetry* (*T.A.S.P.*), a short-lived small-press magazine dedicated to speculative poetry.

In 1984 he edited *Burning with a Vision*, probably the most important commercial anthology in science fiction poetry because it showcased both science fiction and speculative poetry on the same pages.

Ironically he has been nominated many times for the Rhysling, but he won it only once. Too often Frazier poems find themselves competing on the same ballot with other Frazier poems. Finally, it should be said that Robert Frazier has the knack for appearing in publications that are officially closed to poetry.

Commercial Magazine Appearances: *Aboriginal SF*, AMZ, *Analog*, *Fantasy Book*, *Galaxy*, IASFM, F&SF, *Night Cry*, *Weird Tales*

Small-Press Magazine Appearances: *Last Wave*, *New Pathways*, SL

Anthology Appearances: A&L, *Poly*, *1979 Rhysling Anthology*, *1980 Rhysling Anthology*, *1986 Rhysling Anthology*, *1987 Rhysling Anthology*, SFUW, *The Umbral Anthology of Science Fiction Poetry*

Anthologies Written by Writer:
  Co-orbital Moons. Mountain View, CA: Ocean View Press, 1987.
  Perception Barriers. Berkeley, CA: Berkeley Poets Workshop & Press, 1987.

Award: Co-winner, 1980 Rhysling for Short Poem

Friesner, Esther

> 54 Mendingwall Circle
> Madison, CT 06443

Friesner is best known for fantasy adventure novels set in a universe that borrows heavily from "1001 Arabian Nights." Her poetry is also generally fantasy and humor but covers a broader range of fantasy themes. She uses her poetry as entertainment that deflates some of the literary "sacred cows" of fantasy such as chivalry.

Poetry frequently appears in her fantasy novels for a wide range of purposes. From Friesner's point of view it would be inconceivable to describe a universe without poetry. One of the more interesting uses of poetry in novels occurred in her work *The Water King's Laughter* (New York: Avon, 1988). In it she has a poetry contest in which several extremely bad poets enter. As a result, some of the worst poetry conceivable is within the work.

Commercial Magazine Appearances: AMZ, *Fantasy Book*

Froehlich, Joey

> 713 Wilson
> Frankfort, KY 40601

Froehlich has written a prodigious number of poems in the horror genre for both commercial and small-press markets. His poems are short pieces that are nasty and evocative, and leave readers with the feeling that they have been slapped in the face with a taloned claw. Often his language is subtle and not explicitly violent. This only enhances the impact of his work. In truth his poems can be considered the written equivalent of a John Carpenter or Wes Craven film.

In 1983 he edited and published *Whispered Legends* (Frankfort, KY: Weird House), an anthology of poems and prose in the contemporary horror vein. He is currently putting together a sequel anthology, *Violent Legends*, also through his personal imprint of Weird House. In 1978 and 1979 he was briefly the editor of the *Diversifier*, one of the first small-press magazines in the science fiction/fantasy/horror genre.

He has been nominated for the SPWAO, Kelly, and Balrog awards in poetry.

Commercial Magazine Appearance: AMZ

Small-Press Magazine Appearances: *Argonaut, Beyond the Fields We Know, Dark Fantasy, Diversifier, Eldritch Tales, Evermist, Grue, Prelude to Fantasy,* SN, *Twigs*

Garey, Terry

2528 15th Ave., S.
Minneapolis, MN 55404

Garey's voice is strong in science fiction poetry. Her use of short, choppy lines hammers what she wants to say to the reader. Frequently her poems are broken down into self-contained units that have their own structure. She frequently talks about perceptions of the universe from a female perspective, often with erotic elements. Most genre poets are detached when dealing with eroticism in their work, but Garey deals with it head on. She successfully uses it as a tool for looking at the universe.

In 1981 she was nominated for the Rhysling in the Short Poem category. A frequent speaker on poetry and feminism at science fiction conventions, she has been involved in WISCON, a Madison, Wisconsin, convention that deals with feminist issues. She is a former editor of *Aurora*, a fanzine devoted to feminism and poetry. She is currently the poetry editor for the small-press science fiction magazine *Tales of the Unanticipated*.

Small-Press Magazine Appearances: *Magazine of Speculative Poetry, Pacific Northwest Review of Books, Paradox, Princeton Spectrum, Uranus, Velocities*
Anthology Appearances: A&L, BWV, *1982 Rhysling Anthology*

Green, Scott E.

47 Byledge Rd.
Manchester, NH 03104

The bulk of Green's work as a poet has been commentary on the conventions of science fiction, fantasy, and horror. Few of his poems have been narrative.

Green is a relentless spokesman for poetry and has chaired panels on poetry at several World Science Fiction Conventions and North American Science Fiction Conventions as well as running poetry workshops at other conventions.

He is the publisher/editor of *Rising Star,* a newsletter on markets for science fiction, fantasy, and horror writers. He published and edited *Star/Sword Poetry Chapbook I,* a collection of original poetry by new poets in the field. Probably his greatest contribution to genre poetry was persuading the editor of *Amazing* to start buying poetry.

Commercial Magazine Appearances: *Aboriginal SF,* AMZ
Small-Press Magazine Appearances: *Alpha Adventures, American Fantasy, Beyond, Bleeding Virgin, Eldritch Tales, New Pathways, Night Voyage,* OF, PAN, SN, *Space & Time,* SL, Z *Miscellaneous*
Anthology Appearance: A&L
Anthologies Written by Writer:
Private Worlds. Woburn, MA: Beduoin Press, 1983.
Baby Sale at the 7-11. Newark, NJ: Bloom Books, 1985.

Haines, John Francis

5 Cross Farm, Station Road
Padgate
Warrington WA2 OQG
ENGLAND

Haines is an English poet who uses science fiction themes for primarily mainstream markets. In addition he has the added fillip of having his material broadcast on national radio in England (BBC Radio Merseyside). Most of his appearances to date have been in science fiction fanzines or small-press magazines in England. Typically his work combines futuristic themes with traditional forms when he writes science fiction poetry.

Small-Press Magazine Appearances: *New Moon Quarterly,* PM *Poetry Magazine*
Chapbook Written by Writer:
Other Places, Other Times. N.p.: House of Moonlight Press, 1981.

Haldeman, Joe

5412 N. W. 14th Ave.
Gainesville, Fl   32605

Joe Haldeman is one of the preeminent science fiction novelists. His focus has been on military science fiction, a variation of hard science fiction. As its name implies, military science fiction uses future military operations as settings, though its protagonists may not be in the military.

His novels revolve around heroes who are common soldiers caught up in wars that make little sense to them. Since Haldeman is a Vietnam veteran, it's not surprising. His poetry also uses the same theme.

His poem "Saul's Death," which won the 1983 Rhysling for the Long Poem, was a double sestina about an artist who becomes a mercenary and dies in a war. His death was noble but it was sacrificed for an ignoble cause. The poem originally appeared in *Omni*, which listed it as a short story.

He edited *Nebula Awards Stories Seventeen* and initiated the policy by which poems that won the Rhysling appear in the annual anthology of writers who win the SFWA Nebula Awards. This ensures that at least once a year, two or more science fiction poems appear in a commercial anthology. Oddly enough while poetry does appear in his novels, they are not necessary to understanding his work per se.

Haldeman currently teaches writing at M.I.T.

Commercial Magazine Appearances: *Harper's*, IASFM, *Omni*
Small-Press Magazine Appearances: *Pulpsmith*, SL, *Velocities*
Anthology Appearances: BWV, *1984 Rhysling Anthology*
Award: 1983 Rhysling for Long Poem

Hamburger, Michael

c/o Ocean View Press
P. O. Box 4148
Mountain View, CA 94040

Hamburger first came to the notice of the science fiction community as one of the poets appearing in *New Worlds*. His American appearances have been few, primarily in anthologies edited by Judith Merrill such as *England Swings SF*.

Like many of the poets associated with *New Worlds*, his work is speculative rather than science fiction. Much of it is concerned with exploring the reasons why writers write, especially those who write science fiction.

Anthology Appearance: *Poly*

Humphries, Dwight E.

1181 Pine Grove Ave.
Atlanta, GA 30319

Humphries's poems are grim, no matter what genre he writes in. His protagonists despair that their lot in the universe can ever improve. His technical skills as a poet are excellent, but his strong negativism may explain why his work has appeared infrequently.

Currently he operates Triglav Press, an imprint focused on publishing an irregular poetry broadsheet series called *Alatuir*. While not a genre imprint per se, Triglav Press has published horror poetry by Steve Sneyd, Mark Rich, and Wayne Sallee. The poems he publishes tend to be as same as what he writes, cold and well crafted.

Small-Press Magazine Appearances: *Dragonfields, Dreams & Nightmares, Supernatural Poetry*
Anthology Appearance: *Alternate Lives*

Joron, Andrew

P. O. Box 5293
Berkeley, CA 94705

Of all the poets working in the science fiction genre, Andrew Joron is among the best of those who focus on speculative poetry. However, his work is neither cold nor passionless, usually a problem for speculative poets. In much of his work there is a powerful sense of spirituality, a strong conviction that the nature of humanity lies beyond being a mere step in the evolutionary process. It is probably this strong spiritual sense in his work (coupled with fine technical skill) that won him the Rhysling three times, twice for the Long Poem in 1980 and 1986 and as cowinner for the Short Poem in 1978.

He has founded *Velocities,* a small-press magazine that is a major showcase for speculative poetry within the science fiction genre. While many of the major science fiction poets such as Frazier and Boston have written several chapbooks Joron has done only one, *Force Fields,* published by Starmont House, an imprint that normally does academic works on science fiction.

Commercial Magazine Appearances: AMZ, IASFM, *New Worlds*
Small-Press Magazine Appearances: *Magazine of Speculative Poetry, Pig Iron, Portland Review, SN, SL*

Anthology Appearances: BWV, *Poly, 1980 Rhysling Anthology,*
   1982 Rhysling Anthology, 1983 Rhysling Anthology,
   1984 Rhysling Anthology, 1985 Rhysling Anthology, The
   Umbral Anthology of Science Fiction
Chapbook Written by Writer:
   Force Fields. Mercer Island, WA: Starmont House, 1985.
Awards: Rhysling for Long Poem, 1980 and 1986; Cowinner,
   Rhysling for Short Poem, 1978

Kelly, Scott A.

P. O. Box 1030
Bethany, OK 73008

Kelly is an interesting poet, though as yet he has not had many
publications. He is one of those who are interested in having the reader
see what he sees. Most poets would be reluctant to harness the reader's
perception and make the reader see exactly what the poet wants him or
her to see. Kelly readily admits that he writes poetry primarily when
he has a writer's block on his other work.

Commercial Magazine Appearance: AMZ
Small-Press Magazine Appearance: *Byline,* SL

Kenin, Millea

1025 55th St.
Oakland, CA 94608

Active in all three genres as a writer and editor, Kenin's poetry has
been primarily mood pieces set in the horror genre. As editor of the now
dormant *Owlflight* magazine and the *Aliens and Lovers* anthology, her
efforts were major small-press showcases for genre poetry during the
early 1980s.

Small-Press Magazine Appearances: *Hoofstrikes,* SL

Kernaghan, Eileen

5512 Neville St.
Burnaby, BC
CANADA V5J 2H7

Kernaghan is a fantasy novelist as well as a science fiction and
fantasy poet. A feminist and an academic, she has published only in

Canadian academic and feminist publications. Her poems deal with the seeping of magic into the mundane world. Their settings may range from ancient Ur in Sumeria to a forest of photon light trees. Yet her theme remains the same: Magic is an integral part of existence. The source material for her poetry is based firmly on the mythologies of various cultures. It gives an authenticity and power to her work.

Poetry frequently appears in her fantasy novels. They are an integral part of the work, since her fantasy novels are set in a Bronze Age milieu, a period of culture where poems and songs have a significance and power that modern people cannot fully appreciate.

Her poetry also has appeared in the Canadian science fiction anthology *Tesseracts,* edited by Judith Merrill and published by Press Porcepic of Victoria, British Columbia.

Small-Press Magazine Appearances: *Branching Out, Northern Journey, Prism, Room of One's Own.*

Kopaska-Merkel, David

116 First St.
Troy, NY 12180

A geologist, Kopaska-Merkel is best known as the publisher-editor of *Dreams and Nightmares,* a small-press magazine that is one of the few that publishes exclusively fantasy and horror poetry. His publication has focused on what can be described as non-traditional, psychological horror. The poems he uses are cold-blooded and disturbing. For a short time he decided not to pay for poetry and noticed that the quality of the work being submitted fell off.

He is also a fine horror poet in his own right. Like the work he publishes, his own poems are cool pieces of subtle horror. Some may find his work too cool. His poems can appear to be descriptive paragraphs from a Stephen King or Peter Straub novel.

Commercial Magazine Appearance: *Night Cry*
Small-Press Magazine Appearances: *Alphs Adventures, Grue, New Moon, OF, Prelude to Fantasy, SN, SL, Sycophant, 2 A.M.*

Lackey, Mercedes R.

207 S. Harvard
Tulsa, OK 74112

Many poets in the genres have gone on to become prose writers in the field. These would include Steve Rasnic Tem, Bob Frazier, and Jessica Amanda Salmonson. However, Lackey is probably the first writer to have her professional beginnings as a writer and singer of verse, in other words as a professional filksinger.

Lackey was (and remains) an enthusiastic filksinger at many conventions. She recorded two cassettes of her songs for Off-Centaur (*Murder, Mystery and Mayhem*, which was crime-fiction oriented, and *Heralds, Harpers and Havoc*). As a novelist, she has used poems to encapsulate and focus on particularly important moments in her novels.

Commercial Magazine Appearance: *Fantasy Book*

Lee, James A.

801 26th St.
Windber, PA 15963

A free-lance writer who only occasionally dabbles in science fiction poetry. Lee uses hoary space-opera clichés and language to achieve strong emotional responses from the reader. While he may never be a major genre poet, his work proves that considerable power can be distilled from the most stereotypical science fiction themes.

Small-Press Magazine Appearance: *Beyond*
Anthology Appearance: A&L

Le Guin, Ursula K.

c/o Virginia Kidd
Box 278
Milford, PA 18337

The concerns of Le Guin the poet are much the same as Le Guin the novelist. No matter what the genre of her poems (fantasy, science fiction, allegorical, speculative), her characters are frequently pushing themselves to go into the unknown. This hunger is the core of their identity. Her poem "The Well of Baln" won the 1982 Rhysling for Long Poem.

Small-Press Magazine Appearance: SL
Anthology Appearances: BWV, *1980 Rhysling Anthology*
Award: 1982 Rhysling for Long Poem

Leiper, Esther M.

Box 96
Jefferson, NH 03583

Leiper is one of the most successful science fiction/fantasy/ horror poets, though her work rarely appears in genre markets. She is a prolific winner of poetry contests, a source of income that most poets have considerable trouble tapping. Many of her entries have science fiction, fantasy, or horror elements. However, her work goes beyond being an industrious enterer of contests.

Much of her energy is now focused on book-length ballads that employ strictly patterned verse. Her first effort in this direction was *The Wars of Faery*. It was serialized in the poetry magazine *Amelia*. *Wars* was the product of several years' work and was started out of a desire to show that there was still a paying market for work of this nature.

She also serves as poetry editor of Z *Miscellaneous*, a mainstream literary journal that regularly buys much science fiction, fantasy, and horror poetry. Her work as a columnist on poetry for *Writer's Journal* gives her an audience beyond the confines of either genre fans or devotees of poetry contests.

Commercial Magazine Appearance: AMZ
Small-Press Magazine Appearances: OF, *Space & Time*, SL
Anthology Appearance: A&L

Lepovetsky, Lisa

525 N. Michael St.
St. Marys, PA 15857

Lepovetsky is a prolific writer of both prose and poetry for many small-press horror magazines. While her poems do have a nice sense of the nasty, her use of rhyme and structure tends to diminish rather than enhance the reader's sense of horror. Structure has limited her power as a poet.

Small-Press Magazine Appearances: *Dreams & Nightmares, Grue, SN, 2 A.M.*

Lightner, A. M.

Box 174, Birch Rd.
Upper Black Eddy, PA 18972

A. M. Lightner is the maiden name and a pseudonym of prolific science writer Alice L. Hopf. Active as a writer since the late 1920s, she is best known for the nineteen books on science and nature that she has written for the juvenile market under the Hopf byline.

During the 1920s, 1930s, and 1940s she had a minor career as a poet, highlighted by appearances in *American Mercury* and *Nature*. The poem in *Nature* (a now-defunct science magazine) was a piece about the moon, inspired by Ben Johnson's poem, "To Cynthia." Her poem, "To the Moon," grew out of her interest in post–World War II proposals for flights to the moon.

Her own direct work in science fiction poetry appeared in 1965. Her juvenile science fiction novel, *The Galactic Troubador* (New York: Norton, 1965) was about a band of young musicians traveling through the galaxy. In the text of the novel was a considerable body of verse that represented the repertoire of the young heroes. While the novel is now forgotten, it represents an approach by which a science fiction writer integrates poetry and prose in a larger work.

Llewellyn, Alun

52 Silchester Park
Glenageary, Dun Laoghaire
County Dublin, Eire

Llewellyn is best known as a scholar who has specialized in tracing the development of science fiction themes in Western European literature. His own work as a science fiction poet has been a series of poems, collectively called *The Tongues of Zeus*, which examine Man's exploration of the Universe from earliest times. His poems, as well as his science fiction prose have appeared primarily in academic and Celtic nationalist journals.

Small-Press Magazine Appearances: *Irish Science Fiction Journal, Poetry Review of Great Britain*

Lunde, David

252 King Rd.
Forestville, NY 14062

Lunde is a prolific poet. Only part of his output could be considered science fiction.

His career was already well established when he became interested in science fiction themes and concepts via correspondence with Robert Frazier and Gene Van Troyer. Since 1981 his science fiction work has appeared in major outlets. Before 1981, the use of space as a source of imagery was a frequent motif in his work, perhaps because he once worked as a design draftsman in the University of Iowa Department of Physics and Astronomy under Professor James A. Van Allen, the astronomer who discovered the Van Allen radiation belts around the earth during the 1950s.

His style does vary considerably from poem to poem. There always seems to be a sadness to his work, a brief cry over the victims of the impersonal workings of the universe.

Perhaps the greatest attraction that science fiction has for him is the possibility of being published in magazines that have readerships in the hundreds of thousands. In the course of his career he was the poetry editor for the *Riverside Quarterly*, the first serious academic journal devoted to science fiction, fantasy, and horror. He also has the distinction of being one of the few poets published in *Galaxy*.

Lunde is currently writer-in-residence and director of the Creative Writing Program at the State University of New York at Fredonia, editor/publisher of the Basilisk Press, and contributing editor of *Escarpment Magazine*.

Commercial Magazine Appearances: *Aboriginal SF, Galaxy,* IASFM, *New Worlds*
Small-Press Magazine Appearances: *Portland Review,* SL, *Tri-Quarterly*
Anthology Appearances: BWV, *Poly, 1985 Rhysling Anthology, 1987 Rhysling Anthology*

Lundy, Jack

> 1024 Vickburgh SE
> Huntsville, AL 35803

Lundy works hard at bringing a sense of whimsey and lightness to his work. He is concerned with viewing the universe through small things, the flight of butterflies rather than the movement of planets.

While an able and competent poet, he tends to overwrite with strong language in his poems. His use of strong language often buries the light and delicate sense of whimsey he is constructing in his poems. Additionally, Lundy is concerned with creating genuine new myths that ring true and do not come across as a literary artifice. Despite the seeming mutually exclusive directions of his poetry, the voice of his work speaks with true emotion that can compensate for the unwieldy structure of his poems. Currently he is working on several poetry collections including a photo album of science fiction fans with poetry and music.

> Small-Press Magazine Appearance: SL

MacIntyre, F. Gwynplaine

> P. O. Box 2213
> Grand Central Sta.
> New York, NY 10163-2213

Science fiction has always been considered a literature of ideas. Yet, there have always been writers who have placed a higher priority on entertaining the reader with a well-written story than challenging the readers with ideas. MacIntyre has been one writer who has taken this viewpoint and applied to poetry. Almost all his poems have been part of a series called "The Improbable Bestiary." Since 1980 "The Improbable Bestiary" has been long, strong poems about the various creatures that inhabit science fiction, fantasy, and horror genres (Yeti, BEM, Ghoul). The poems are characterized by a strong sense of rhyme and structure. Appearing originally in *Isaac Asimov's*, the series migrated to *Amazing* and is now in the often revived *Weird Tales*.

MacIntyre is one poet who makes no bones about writing for the needs of his markets. Most poets are reluctant to sacrifice what they perceive as "artistic integrity" in order to achieve a sale. Not so with

MacIntyre, who feels that professional editors would recognize the commercial value of poetry if poets are responsive to their needs. Curiously he rarely uses verse within the context of his science fiction prose.

It seems that MacIntyre may become the great humorist in science fiction, fantasy, and horror poetry — a suitable role for one who counts Dr. Seuss and Rodgers and Hammerstein as major influences on his work.

Commercial Magazine Appearances: AMZ, IASFM, *Weird Tales*
Small-Press Magazine Appearance: *Raven*
Anthology Appearance: *1981 Rhysling Anthology*

Maggiano, Ron

4020 Carmel Brooks Way
San Diego, CA 92130

Maggiano, a teacher, is interested in science fiction and science poetry as a teaching tool. However, most of his work is dark pieces that reflect a weariness that surpasses definition. This mood is reminiscent of Jack Vance's "Dying Earth" stories and other works set in a far future where science and history have been forgotten.

Small-Press Magazine Appearances: *Cerulean Press Mini-Anthology Series, Dan River Anthology, Encore, Little Magazine, North Country Entertainer, SL, Writer's Haven Journal*
Chapbook Written by Writer:
Moonlight Sonata. San Diego, CA: Ursus Press, 1987

Malcohn, Elissa

P. O. Box 1764
Cambridge, MA 02238

Malcohn loves to use juxtaposition of various metaphors in her work as a poet. The science fiction, fantasy, and horror genre gives her more opportunity to do this. Like so many other poets, she came into the genres because of this flexibility.

She served as editor of *Star*Line*, the newsletter of the Science Fiction Poetry Association. While she claimed that she knew what she was looking for in a poem when she saw it, the editor in her looked for poems that were consistent in structure and that delivered what they promised to do. The same can be said of Malcohn's own work.

Previously she has written as Elissa Hamilton.

Commercial Magazine Appearances: *Aboriginal SF,* AMZ, IASFM
Small-Press Magazine Appearances: *Magazine of Speculative Poetry,* SN, SL
Anthology Appearances: BWV, *1982 Rhysling Anthology, 1983 Rhysling Anthology, 1984 Rhysling Anthology, 1986 Rhysling Anthology*

Marcus, Adrianne

165 Alpine Terrace
San Francisco, CA 94117

Marcus has always been one of those poets who have written poems primarily about science rather than poems of science fiction. Like most successful science poets, she can integrate laws of natural phenomena with the personal concerns expressed by the narrative voice of the poem. This is critical, as many science poems seem impersonal. In those poems, a coldness moves through the reader because the poets seem intent on eliminating the human element from their work. Perhaps they find it necessary in order to emphasize the fact that this is a "science poem." This is a trap that Marcus does not fall into. Her work reflects the observation that a poem without the human element is merely an orderly jumble of words.

Marcus works full time as a free-lance food and travel writer.

In 1982 she was nominated for the Rhysling for Short Poem.

Commercial Magazine Appearances: *Nation, Scientific American*
Small-Press Magazine Appearances: *Appalachian Review, Red Start Quarterly, Rocket Candy*
Anthology Appearances: BWV, *The Umbral Anthology of Science Fiction Poetry, 1982 Rhysling Anthology*
Chapbooks Written by Writer:
   Child of Earthquake Country. San Francisco: Self-published, 1980.
   Faced with Love. Providence, RI: Copper Beech Press, Brown University, 1978

Marra, Sue

Box 206
Westtown, PA 19495-0206

A horror writer whose prose and poetry has appeared in small-press markets, Marra regards mainstream poets' effects to be attempts at describing an orderly, predictable universe. She feels that her own work as a poet reflects the universe as it is, a crazy, subjective place. Much of her work has appeared in fanzines.

Small-Press Magazine Appearances: *Arcane, 2 A.M.,* SL

Mayer, Frederick J.

429 E. Bijou #2-C
Colorado Springs, CO 80903

Frederick Mayer is one of those responsible for the present structure of the community of poets active within the science fiction, fantasy, and horror genres. As a poet he has argued for the need of science fiction poets to develop new forms. However, most of his own work could be loosely described as fantasy or horror. For those two genres Mayer has commented that fantasy and horror poetry must shed the "hackneyed gothic" themes that are part of it. While many poets would agree with Mayer's point, they find his arguments daunting and intimidating.

On a more practical level, Mayer has pioneered the development of science fiction convention poetry programs (both readings and panels) since 1978. It cannot be overstated that the convention is the principal medium by which the science fiction/fantasy/horror community of fans and professionals interact with each other. The convention becomes a showcase where new ideas are discussed and old ones are redefined. The fact that conventions had poetry programming was proof to the fan that poetry was a legitimate form of expression in science fiction, fantasy, and horror. While poetry programs did precede Mayer's activities, they were minor efforts that had little impact on the field. Mayer persuaded (in 1978) the organizers of the World Science Fiction Convention to include a poetry panel. Since that time poetry programming has become a regular part of conventions. The importance of these panels cannot be exaggerated. They are one of the few forums that allow poets, readers, and editors actually to meet each other.

As an editor, Mayer put together retrospective anthologies of the work by H. Warner Munn and Joseph Payne Brenan as well as the

Fantasy Editor of *T.A.S.P.*, a short-lived speculative poetry magazine founded by Robert Frazier.

In the last few years much of his work as a poet has been devoted to performing his poetry. His magazine appearances have been few in recent years. Mayer has been nominated for the Rhysling, the Balrog (a short-lived award that included poetry among its categories), and the International Clark Ashton Smith Award (CLASH), which he won in 1983. The CLASH was founded by Mayer in 1979 in conjunction with Fantasy Faire, a now-defunct California convention. Like the Rhysling, it was intended to honor science fiction and fantasy poetry. The awards were dropped when the organizers of Fantasy Faire let the annual convention lapse.

Small-Press Magazine Appearances: *Eldritch Tales, Grue*, SL
Anthology Appearance: *1981 Rhysling Anthology*

Mayhar, Ardath

P. O. Box 180
Chireno, TX 75937

Mayhar started her writing career as a mainstream poet, turned to fantasy, horror, and science fiction prose, and has now become a genre poet. Her poems tend to be long narratives. There is always a strong sense of conflict in her poetry that is muffled in her prose. In 1984 she won the Balrog for poetry.

Commercial Magazine Appearances: *Fantasy Book, Fantasy Review*
Small-Press Magazine Appearances: *Borderland, Eldritch Tales, Grue, Tempest*
Award: 1984 Balrog

Moffett, Judith

39 Rabbit Run
Wallingford, PA 19086

Moffett is a University of Pennsylvania English professor who did not start out to write science fiction poetry. Like so many others, she has found it to be an appropriate forum for her work. Her poetry focuses on human evolution and the linguistic research being done with apes.

Currently most of her genre appearances consist of excerpts from one long poem, "Missing Link."

Commercial Magazine Appearance: IASFM

Small-Press Magazine Appearances: *Kenyon Review, Michigan Quarterly Review*

Chapbooks Written by Writer:

Keeping Time. Baton Rouge: Louisiana State University Press, 1970.

Whinny Moor Crossing. Princeton, NJ: Princeton University Press, 1984.

Morgan, Edwin

19 Whittingehame Court
Glasgow G12 0BG
SCOTLAND

Morgan, a former academic, is not typical of the British poets who have written science fiction poetry. First, he generally writes narrative poems set in a non-terrestrial setting rather than poems about science. Most of the major British poets in the science fiction genre focus on poems about science. Second, he is not one of the British poets strongly identified with *New Worlds*.

Unlike so many British genre poets he makes no bones about being a science fiction fan. For him the appeal of science fiction has always been its juxtaposing of art and science whether it be poetry, prose, or even film. He uses poetry as a means to link science and the everyday human experience. Even in poems that technically are just poems about science, he injects a strong narrative sense that links the reader with poems and thus infuses it with the power of a tale.

Four of his chapbooks had a significant portion of science fiction poetry. He has also appeared in three major science fiction poetry anthologies, one of which, *Frontier of Going* (edited by John Fairfax; London: Panther Books, 1969) has not appeared in the United States.

In Britain the attempt to classify writers and their work by genre has not been a problem. Writers are less likely to suffer from having their work viewed or published according to narrow definitions. It seems doubtful that Edwin Morgan would have enjoyed such success and acceptance if his career had started in America.

Anthology Appearances: BWV, HYEH

Chapbooks Written by Writer:
From the Video Box. Glasgow: Mariscat Press, 1986.
Poems of Thirty Years. Manchester, England: Carcanet Press, 1982.
Sonnets from Scotland. Glasgow: Mariscat Press, 1984.
Star Gate. Glasgow: Third Eye, 1979.

Morlan, A. R.

608 E. 11th St., S.
Ladysmith, WI 54848-2030

Horror in any form is Morlan's medium. To Morlan, poetry is an important alternative to the short story. The writer can hammer home a particular idea to the reader. The mechanics of a good short story may only serve to diminish the impact of ideas. However, Morlan does not scorn prose. She has many horror short story sales including appearances in *Twilight Zone* and *Night Cry.* Her poetry appearances to date are few. Nevertheless, her poems have received critical attention because she is not shy to immerse the reader in horror. "What the Janitor Found," a poem based on several actual infanticide cases, received nominations for the SFWA Nebula Short Story category and the Stoker Awards of Horror Writers of America.

Commercial Magazine Appearance: *Night Cry*
Small-Press Magazine Appearance: SL

Mycue, Edward

P. O. Box 640543
San Francisco, CA 94164-0543

It is hard to describe a Mycue poem except that it is polished and professional. Mycue is a voluminous writer, and there is no distinctive Mycue style. To some the fact that one Mycue poem is unlike any other Mycue poem is a source of praise. Others would say that is a sign of a hack, a criticism that literary critics are always imposing on genre writers.

Unlike many of his peers, Mycue has had some publishing success with chapbooks, an area of publishing that few genre poets seem to get into. All his chapbooks contain science fiction and fantasy poetry.

Small-Press Magazine Appearances: *Macabre, Nightmares of Reason*, PAN, *Riverside Quarterly*, SL, *Star Wine, Velocities*
Anthology Appearances: *Poly, A Walk in the Dark*
Chapbooks Written by Writer:
Damage Within the Community. Los Angeles: Panjandrum Press, 1973.
Edward. Cambridge, MA: Primal Publishing, 1987.
Route, Route and Range: The Song Returns. Melbourne, Australia: Paper Castle, 1979.
Since We Speak. Peterborough, Cambridgeshire, England: Spectacular Diseases Press, 1988.
The Singing Man My Father Gave Me. London: Menard Press, 1980.

Palwick, Susan

260 Engle St., #3-1
Englewood, NJ 07631

A full-time professional writer, Palwick started writing science fiction poetry for one simple reason: She saw a science fiction poem in *Amazing* and thought she could do better. Her estimate of her work was obviously correct, since she has sold to both *Amazing* and *Isaac Asimov*. She also won the 1985 Rhysling for Short Poetry.

Palwick's views on poetry and science fiction are derived from Samuel Delaney's comments in *The Jewel-Hinged Jaw.* Like Delaney she believes that science fiction and poetry mix well, since they attempt to describe the world without reproducing it. They both also demand that the reader be able and willing to interpret metaphors.

Stylistically her poems fall into two groups, both marked by formal structure. One is quotellas, poems based on quotes in prose or nonfiction works. The other is narrative ballads. She is currently an editor with the *Little Magazine.*

Commercial Magazine Appearances: AMZ, IASFM
Anthology Appearance: *1985 Rhysling Anthology*
Award: 1985 Rhysling Short Poem

Payack, Peter

64 Highland Ave.
Cambridge, MA 02139

Payack always seems to be having a good time when he writes poetry. Most of his work is light-hearted while at the same time speaks about important themes. The problem is that Payack is chuckling at you while you are reading it. You want to take Payack seriously, but do you dare? Payack founded Phone-A-Poem in Boston, an endeavor that has bought poetry from some science fiction poets. In 1980 he co-won the Rhysling for Short Poem.

Commercial Magazine Appearances: AMZ, IASFM
Small-Press Magazine Appearance: SL
Anthology Appearances: BWV, *1980 Rhysling Anthology, The Umbral Anthology of Science Fiction*
Award: 1980 cowinner, Rhysling for Short Poem

Pelegrimas, Marthayn

5116 S. 143 St.
Omaha, NE 68137

While she writes poems in all three genres, science fiction/ fantasy/horror, Pelegrimas's works share common elements. Like that of many genre poets, her work is disciplined and structured. Rhymes, meter, and line structure are always important. Equally important is the use of the twist ending in her poems, a reflection of an early appetite for "Twilight Zone," "Alfred Hitchcock Presents," and Saturday matinee horror movies. Not surprisingly, Pelegrimas regards Rod Serling as her major literary influence.

Commercial Magazine Appearance: *Omaha Magazine*
Small-Press Magazine Appearances: *Gas, Suicide Notes, Sycophant, Thin Ice, Twisted, 2 A.M.*

Pilkington, Ace

P. O. Box 1257
St. George, UT 84770

Pilkington's poems talk about individuals and their perceptions of their universe. Then he uses his characters' perceptions as a means of describing the metaphorical truth. A Shakespearean scholar, Pilkington uses language and structure that are reminiscent of the great English poets and playwrights such as Shakespeare and Keats.

Commercial Magazine Appearances: AMZ, IASFM, *Weird Tales*
Small-Press Magazine Appearances: *Orbis, Poetry Wales, Z Miscellaneous*

Post, Jonathan

385 S. Catalina #231
Pasadena, CA 91106-3353

Post's voice is harsh and powerful in his poetry. While he has done work in fantasy and horror, science fiction and science poems are his meat. There is a cold impersonality to his work that roars at the reader. This coldness is a metaphor for the last and indifferent universe that surrounds us. In spite of his work's coldness, his technical skills as a poet have engaged the admiration of his peers as well as several Rhysling nominations.

Commercial Magazine Appearances: AMZ, *Fantasy Book*
Small-Press Magazine Appearance: SL
Anthology Appearances: BWV, *Lost Lands, Poly, 1985 Rhysling Anthology, 1986 Rhysling Anthology, 1987 Rhysling Anthology*

Rantala, Kathryn

1212 8th N.
Edmonds, WA 98020

Rantala is a mainstream poet who moved to science fiction poetry because she perceived mainstream poetry as safe and predictable. Science fiction poetry had that vitality and daring that she felt is necessary for the work of poets. The exchange among science fiction poets is what keeps her in the genre and is a source of personal pleasure to her. This interchange among writers has always been an important part of science fiction writing. Curiously, her poetry tends to be highly structured and well written but remote to the reader. The excitement that Rantala finds important in science fiction poetry does not come through well in her work. Perhaps it is this coolness in her otherwise excellent work that has given her several Rhysling nominations but never the award itself.

Small-Press Magazine Appearances: *Speculative Poetry Review*, SL

Anthology Appearances: BWV, *Poly*, *1978 Rhysling Anthology*, *1982 Rhysling Anthology*, *The Umbral Anthology of Science Fiction Poetry*

Rathbone, Wendy

14156 Tobiasson Rd.
Poway, CA 92064

While she works in all three genres, Rathbone's poems always seem to be steeped in a deep sense of horror. Her work is dominated by an obsessive search for defining humanity's place in the universe. This is not uncommon. Many poets work this theme, but the language tends to be overwritten, à la Lovecraft. Rathbone's work avoids these pitfalls. When Rathbone was young, she suffered from recurrent nightmares. Perhaps the memory of those nightmares crept into her work to give it that distinctive dark quality.

Commercial Magazine Appearances: *Aboriginal SF*
Small-Press Magazine Appearances: *Pandora*, SL, *Z Miscellaneous*

Rawls, Melanie A.

1412 Orange St.
Thomasville, GA 31792

High fantasy has been this poet's forte. Her work as a fantasy poet has focused on new perspectives of traditional European fairy tales. She is also active as a scholar in the field of high fantasy. Her scholarly work has appeared in *Mythlore* and *Mythprint*, publications of the Mythopoeic Society, a scholarly group dedicated to the study of the work of J.R.R. Tolkien, C. S. Lewis, and Charles Williams.

Small-Press Magazine Appearances: *Mythlore*, SL

Raz, Jonathan

1814 Arch St.
Berkeley, CA 94709

Not particularly prolific, Raz has written love poems nestled within science fiction poems. His poems are truly both science fiction and romantic, since both components are needed for his poems to go beyond mere description of phenomena or emotion and work as poems. While genre poets are comfortable with romance, Raz has made love his own particular specialty in science fiction poetry.

Small-Press Magazine Appearances: *Alba, Blue Unicorn, Berkeley Poetry Review, SL, T.A.S.P., Velocities*

Redgrove, Peter

c/o Ocean View Press
P. O. Box 4148
Mountain View, CA 94040

Redgrove is best known to the American science fiction community for his work in *New Worlds* and *England Swings SF*. Considered one of the major speculative poets, his current work is an interesting merger. He has natural and scientific phenomena described as manifestations of the metaphysical world. In fact Redgrove makes no distinction between the physical and the spiritual universe. It is just a matter of perception by individuals choosing to see what they want to see. In Redgrove's universe, the only sure law is Heisenberg's Principle of Uncertainty.

Commercial Magazine Appearances: *Atlantic Monthly, New Worlds*
Small-Press Magazine Appearances: *Antaeus, Manhattan Review*
Anthology Appearances: *England Swings SF*, HYEH, *Poly*

Rentz, Jr., Thomas A.

1022 Chandlar St.
Eagle River, AK 99577

Rentz is a prolific poet whose work has been largely confined to genre small-press magazines and anthologies. His work is competent but hard to categorize because there is no recurrent theme or structure to his output. Except for an appearance in the now-defunct *Fantasy Review*, his only major commercial appearances have been poems in *Humpty Dumpty* and *Children's Playmate*. His sales to major children's markets highlight a curious fact. Children's magazines should be logical markets for genre poets, but only Rentz seems to be able to crack this large and profitable market.

Commercial Magazine Appearances: *Children's Playmate, Humpty Dumpty*
Small-Press Magazine Appearances: *Alpha Adventures, Beyond, Fantasy Review,* SN, SL
Anthology Appearance: *Alternate Lives*

Rich, Mark

P. O. Box 564
Beloit, WI 53511

Rich is best known as the copublisher and coeditor of the *Magazine of Speculative Poetry*. From 1974 to 1976, he was the coeditor of *Treaders of Starlight*, a major early showcase for science fiction poetry. His own poetry is generally elegant, highly structured descriptions of various aspects of space exploration, especially concerning exploring new worlds.

Commercial Magazine Appearances: AMZ, *Fantasy Review*
Small-Press Magazine Appearances: PAN, SL, *Uranus, Visions*
Anthology Appearances: *Alternate Lives, Poly, 1986 Rhysling Anthology*

Riley, Tom

Department of English
Canisius College
Buffalo, NY 14208

A college English instructor, Riley has always been a science fiction fan. When he started writing poetry, it just came out science fiction. His poems tend to be long pieces that decry the materialism that plagues twentieth-century America. They also harken back to major poets such as Dante in their precise description of individuals.

Commercial Magazine Appearance: *Buffalo News*
Small-Press Magazine Appearances: *The Lyric,* SL

Rosenman, John B.

Department of English
Norfolk State University
Norfolk, VA 23504

Rosenman is a horror writer equally comfortable in either prose or poetry. While his work as a short story writer is better known, Rosenman's poetry is attracting attention, though it has not appeared in major showcases. Fear is the one emotion in his work that he attempts to inflict on the reader. To him the power of fear is so strong that it is the equivalent of a major religious experience. An assistant professor of creative writing at Norfolk State University in Virginia, he also worked in mainstream and science fiction prose.

Small-Press Magazine Appearance: *Haunts*

Rothman, Chuck

2012 Pyle Rod.
Schenectady, NY 12303

Rothman, the spouse of Susan Rothman, focuses his attention on science fiction prose. His work in poetry consists of short, humorous pieces poking fun at hoary science fiction clichés.

Small-Press Magazine Appearance: SL

Rothman, Susan Noe

2012 Pule Rd.
Schenectady, NY 12303

Rothman turned to science fiction poetry because her work as a poet started to focus on science fiction themes. While a science fiction fan, she did not start out to write poetry of this type. It just happened. Her poetry is sentimental, evoking a sense of homeliness, which can best be described as poems for some twenty-third century issue of *Redbook* or *Good Housekeeping*. Her sentimentality tends to overwhelm her work.

Commercial Magazine Appearance: *Aboriginal SF*
Small-Press Magazine Appearance: SL

Rutherford, Brett

> 255 Transit St.
> Providence, RI 02906

Rutherford is a great admirer of classic American horror fiction, especially the prose and poetry of H. P. Lovecraft. Like that of Lovecraft, his poetry is traditional in structure and deals with themes that are purely supernatural. Rutherford is not a subtle writer. His style may seem antiquated and his themes may seem hackneyed to some readers. Perhaps the best way to appreciate a Rutherford poem is to think of it as a homage to traditional horror stories.

> Small-Press Magazine Appearances: *Beyond, Haunts*
> Anthology Written by Writer:
>> *Whippoorwill Road.* Providence, RI: The Poet's Press, 1985.

Sallee, Wayne Allen

> 3909 West 85th St., 2nd floor
> Chicago, IL 60652-3730

Sallee started out writing poetry in all three genres but in the last few years has focused on horror. This has been successful for the Chicago writer, since he has had several hundred horror prose and poetry pieces published in small-press and commercial publications. As a poet, his work has been primarily contemporary horror with a focus on psychological rather than supernatural terror. Sallee intends that his poetry be a chronicle of the times he lives in. His unpublished novel, *Paingrin,* is primarily a prose poem that chronicles his daily trials of dealing with a physically crippling disease.

> Small-Press Magazine Appearances: *Deathrealm, Dreams &*
>> *Nightmares, Grue, Haunts,* SN, SL, *Third Lung Review,* Z
>> *Miscellaneous*

Sanders, Debra F.

> 1415 Victoria St., #206
> Honolulu, HI 96822

Sanders is a filksinger who has written for three of Off-Centaur's cassette tapes, "Where No Man . . . ," "Free Fall and Other Delights," and "The Final Frontier." In addition she had material recorded for DAG Productions and Wail Songs. In many ways Sanders is the archetypical filksong writer. Her work is optimistic and positive about the future of humanity in space. Equally obvious is the influence of the "Star Trek" TV series on her work. Her other work as a poet has appeared only in amateur poetry publications.

Satter, Marlene Y.

P. O. Box 715
Salem, AR 72576

Satter is one of those writers who is comfortable in all three genres plus mysteries. Both her prose and her poetry tend to be strong narratives. In both cases she is a storyteller talking directly to the reader. Not surprisingly she prefers to use traditional structure in her poetry. Like so many genre writers evoking a sense of wonder is the most important element in her work. She is one of the few poets who had their work produced on radio. In this instance, the Heart of the Ozarks Theater Company of West Plains, Missouri, did a choral reading of a macabre poem on their "H.O.T. Radio Playhouse" on June 4 and 7, 1987. Satter also writes as Lee Barwood.

Commercial Magazine Appearance: *Fantasy Book*
Small-Press Magazine Appearances: *Space & Time, Undinal Songs, Weird Book*

Schein, Lorraine

41–30 46th St., #5A
Sunnyside, NY 11104

Schein is a curious anomaly in science fiction poetry. Schein is a feminist as are many women science fiction poets (and prose writers, as well). Her work consciously employs feminist components, something that is not typical in science fiction poetry though it is in contemporary science fiction prose as well as fantasy. To her, feminism is the same as any other visionary image. Therefore, it belongs in science fiction poetry. While not just a science fiction poet, she employs fantastic and unusual imaginative elements. To her the greatest flaw of mainstream poetry is a lack of imagination, which makes it technically perfect and emotionally sterile. She is one of the few poets to attend the Clarion

Science Fiction Writer's Workshop, a major incubator of science fiction professionals. Despite the presence of Robert Frazier on the staff, its curriculum pays little attention to poetry. While she attended Clarion in 1980, only now has her prose started to appear. Despite the high quality of her work, she does not have the critical attention due her, probably because most of her work is in small mainstream literary magazines.

Small-Press Magazine Appearances: *Heresies, New York Quarterly, Public Illumination, Semsotexte*, SL, Z *Miscellaneous*

Schwader, Ann K.

8901 Huron St., #206-D
Thornton, CO 80221

Schwader works comfortably in all three genres. Most of her work is in these three areas. A particularly attractive element of working in the genres for her is the camaraderie among the poets. This camaraderie is something that is found among genre prose writers. Many science fiction, fantasy, and horror writers keep active in the field because of this camaraderie. She takes pride in her ability to be a writer who entertains. Yet it does not stop her from using the complex structures associated with speculative poets whose work is introspective.

Commercial Magazine Appearances: *Aboriginal SF*, IASFM
Small-Press Magazine Appearances: *Dreams & Nightmares*, OF, PAN, *Prisoners of the Night*, SN, SL, *The Women's List*

Schweitzer, Darrell

c/o Terminus Publishing Co., Inc.
P. O. Box 13418
Philadelphia, PA   19101-3418

Schweitzer is one of those writers who writes primarily prose with only an occasional poem to his credit, perhaps because Schweitzer, a very able writer of fantasy and horror, uses poetry to express ideas or images that won't work in other forms. Since he is an articulate, skillful writer, he need not resort to poetry often for the expression of ideas. However, he is not above doing a limerick or two because he cannot resist a good joke. A Schweitzer poem always fits perfectly the dictionary description of whatever form it uses, be it limerick or sonnet. Schweitzer is also an editor for the latest incarnation of *Weird Tales,* a magazine that throughout its long if interrupted career has been a major showcase of fantasy and horror poetry.

Commercial Magazine Appearances: AMZ, *Fantasy Book*
Small-Press Magazine Appearances: *Eternity, Fantasy Tales, Mythlore, Speculative Poetry, Review, Weird Book*

Shepard, Lucius

c/o Ace Books
200 Madison Ave.
New York, NY 10016

Lucius Shepard has carved a reputation for himself as a science fiction prose writer whose work combines both searing commentary upon America's foreign policy and an intense narrative voice. These two features also distinguish the occasional poem he has written and has already brought him critical acclaim from other science fiction poets. He is one of the few writers to have sold poetry to *Omni,* a magazine that insists that it does not buy poetry.

Commercial Magazine Appearances: IASFM, *Nightcry, Omni*

Shires, Ian

17914 N. Inlet Dr.
Strongsville, OH 44136

Shires is the publisher/editor of *Mysterious Visions Anthology,* a small-press monthly comic book. At first he published his own poems in the magazine but has now started to buy poems from other writers. While science fiction/fantasy/horror prose and comic books have had a close relationship, what Shires is doing with genre poetry and comics is unique. His own work as a poet is short, straightforward genre pieces that are short tales and lend themselves to illustration.

Sidney-Fryer, Donald

P. O. Box 188701
Sacramento, CA 95818

Sidney-Fryer is both a professional actor and poet. Most of his acting career has been devoted to dramatic readings of the poetry of Edmund Spenser as well as other poets, some of whom belong within the fantasy genre such as Clark Ashton Smith and Ambrose Bierce. His contribution to science fiction/fantasy/horror poetry has been as an editor. Between 1965 and 1980 he edited six volumes of poetry by major fantasy writers. Most of his energy has been devoted to Clark Ashton Smith, but he has edited volumes of the poetry of Robert E. Howard and Ambrose Bierce. The Smith collections were:

Poems in Prose. Sauk City, WI: Arkham House, 1965.
Other Dimensions. Sauk City, WI: Arkham House, 1970.
Selected Poems. Sauk City, WI: Arkham House, 1971.
The Black Book of Clark Ashton Smith (coedited with Ron Hossman). Sauk City, WI: Arkham House, 1977.

The Howard collection was:

Etchings in Ivory. Pasadena, TX: Glenn Lord, 1968.

The Bierce Collection was:

A Vision of Doom. West Kingston, RI: Donald M. Grant, 1978.

As a science fiction/fantasy/horror poet, most of his original work has focused on the Atlantean myth. The poems have been collected in an Arkham House volume. It should come as no great surprise that Sidney-Fryer's style should be Elizabethean in language and structure.

Commercial Magazine Appearance: *Witchcraft & Sorcery*
Anthology Written by Writer:
Songs and Sonnets Atlantean. Sauk City, WI: Arkham House, 1971.

Simon, John Oliver

c/o California Poets in the Schools
Department of English
University of California
Berkeley, CA 94720

Simon's poems frequently start in the idealized past (usually with a Latin American flavor), and then by slow increments they become set in the future. Most times the narrators of his poems are individuals who are acutely aware of the distant past and the distant future. The present in which they function is a fleeting moment that the gods and nature conspire to dole out to humans. Simon is the editor of the mainstream small-press imprint *Aldebaran Review*.

Small-Press Magazine Appearances: *Abraxes, Chelsea, Magazine of Speculative Poetry, Poetry Northwest, Prairie Schooner*, SL, *Velocities*
Anthology Appearances: BWV, *Poly*

Simon, Marge

1412 N. E. 35th St
Ocala, FL 32670

An artist as well as a writer of prose and poetry, Simon has developed within the small-press segment of science fiction/fantasy/horror markets. Like so many genre professionals whose roots lie in small press, she has been active in the Small Press Writers and Artists Organization (SPWAO) and honed her skills as a writer within its various in-house publications. Many prose writers who start to experiment with poetry had their early efforts published in the *SPWAO Newsletter*, and Simon was no exception. At the same time she appeared in fanzines, she started to crack the major markets. Ironically her art but not her poetry has appeared in *Star*Line*. As a poet her work embodies elements from all three genres. Her poems can never be described as just "science fiction" or "horror" or "fantasy." Simon generally uses a formal structure in her work, an interesting contrast to her flexible attitude toward imagery.

Commercial Magazine Appearance: AMZ
Small-Press Magazine Appearances: *Beyond, Hoofstrikes, Minnesota Fantasy Review, Ouroboros*, SN, *Thin Ice, Twisted*

Simpson, Don

977 Kains Ave.
Albany, CA 94706

Simpson is one of the original staff members of Off-Centaur Publications. Off-Centaur is also his principal publisher for verse. While his work ranges through all three genres, the bulk of it is based on traditional folklore and legends. Stylistically he is conservative as would be expected of any poet whose work would be set to music. Currently he is putting together an anthology of erotic poems about centaurs.

Skov, David M.

4851 Irvine Ave.
N. Hollywood, CA 91601-4318

David Skov is a poet whose career is known almost entirely from his small-press appearances. Writing also as D. M. Vosk and as Dewi McS, he shows an admirable talent of writing to the needs of every publication in which he has appeared. Skov's particular skill is in writing short, intense poems that hammer one strong emotion to the reader.

Small-Press Magazine Appearances: *Beyond*, OF, SN, SL, 2 *A.M.*
Anthology Appearances: AL, *1987 Rhysling Anthology*

Sladek, John

c/o Richard Curtis Assoc.
164 E. 64th St.
New York, NY 10021

Sladek is one of science fiction's preeminent satirists. Poetry does appear in his novels as minor embellishments. Other than that, his only poems have appeared in *Holding Your Eight Hands*. In 1969 and 1970 he was coeditor of the short-lived *Ronald Reagan: The Magazine of Poetry* in London. While not a science fiction publication per se, it published speculative poetry by such writers as J. G. Ballard, Michael Moorcock, and Thomas M. Disch.

Anthology Appearance: HYEH

Sneyd, Steve

Hilltop, 4 Nowell Pl.
Almondsbury, Huddersfield
West Yorkshire, HD5 8PB
ENGLAND

Steve Sneyd is one of the few English writers who regularly appear in American markets. His work reflects a rather dry English humor. However, that humor frequently has a dark side to it. Additionally, Sneyd's work often displays a negative view of man struggling in a large, impersonal universe. If they featured poetry on "Monty Python," Sneyd would have written it.

Commercial Magazine Appearances: *Dreams & Nightmares, Magazine of Speculative Poetry,* OF, SN, SL
Anthology Appearances: AL, BWV, *The Umbral Anthology of Science Fiction Poetry*

Spangle, Douglas

1315 S. E. 48th
Portland, OR 97206

Spangle does not set out to write science fiction/fantasy poetry per se, but since he is a fan of those two genres, their conventions and themes appear in his work. Interestingly enough he is also an admirer of romantic literature. Thus his work also has a strong romantic flavor that is not associated with science fiction or fantasy poetry. He can be best compared to the 1930s adventure novelist Rafael Sabatini who blended sword fighting and boudoir adventures in fast-paced novels.

Small-Press Magazine Appearances: *Northwest Review,* SL

Springer, Nancy

360 W. Main St.
Dallastown, PA 17313

Nancy Springer is one of the leading writers of high fantasy, that subgenre of fantasy in which protagonists undergo adverse circumstances and thus acquire a more perfect knowledge of themselves and their place in the universe. In high fantasy, magic is a means by which this discovery is attained. It is not another prop for heavily muscled heroes to vanquish villains. Her poems also generally fall into the high fantasy form. Their style is smooth and elegant. Yet the poems' narrators can be angry, fearful characters. Her poems frequently focus on the terror and pain that can be engendered by a growing self-awareness. This is a theme that is also a central part in her prose. The preciousness that often blights high fantasy is not to be found in her work. Poems are frequently integrated into her novels, either as chapter headings or as songs sung by the novels' characters. The poems are means by which Springer tells the reader about a character's frame of mind or, more commonly, events that predate the lives of the characters. Her unsentimental approach to high fantasy poetry garnered her one Rhysling nomination for Long Poem in 1982.

Not surprisingly, many of her poems have appeared in *Fantasy Book*, a now-suspended magazine that was an important showcase of high fantasy.

Commercial Magazine Appearances: *Fantasy Book, Weird Tales*
Small-Press Magazine Appearances: *Echoes, Night Voyages Poetry Review*, SL
Anthology Appearances: BWV, *1983 Rhysling Anthology*

Stafford, William

c/o Ocean View Press
P. O. Box 4148
Mountain View, CA 94040

Stafford is one of America's leading poets. Some of his recent work has been speculative poems that use science and science fiction themes to explore the human condition, the permanent task of poets. Stafford is not becoming a "science fiction" poet. Rather, he uses science fiction themes as one of his many tools. He is very much aware of poetry's role to fuse art and science into one coherent voice. His poetry is probably the best that any American poet has written in this century. Yet, it seems too dependent on his eruditeness. Poems are teaching tools, but Stafford is too intent on the teaching function in his speculative poetry.

Small-Press Magazine Appearance: SL
Anthology Appearances: SFUM, *The Umbral Anthology of Science Fiction Poetry*

Starkey, David

P. O. Box 171
Blacksburg, VA 24063-0171

A horror writer in both prose and poetry, Starkey writes unsubtle pieces that make it clear to readers what exactly he is saying to them. Metaphors are not a part of this writer's literary tools. His work is grim, grim enough sometimes to overwhelm the high technical quality of his work.

Small-Press Magazine Appearances: *Grue, Wiggensnatch, Z Miscellaneous*
Anthology Appearance: *A Walk in the Dark*

Stearns, Stephanie

3980 W. Radcliff
Denver, CO 80236

Stearns is the writer of many competently crafted poems in all three genres. The bulk of her poetry has appeared in nonpaying showcases and fanzines. Even though she has won the SPWAO Best Poet Award several times, her significance to the field lies not in her poetry but in the work she has done with Small Press Writers and Artists Organization (SPWAO).

Briefly, SPWAO is the principal organization of the three genres that seeks to upgrade the standards of genre small-press publications and provide support service for the editors, writers, and artists who are its members. It also seeks to ensure that small-press publications are recognized as being important in their own right to writers and not a "minor league" for professionals waiting to break into "major league" commercial newsstand magazines.

For any poet, small-press magazines constitute the bulk of their publications, and the importance of SPWAO can never be over-estimated. Much of its work has been through its newsletter, which Stearns has ably edited off and on over the past several years. She has played a large role to make sure that SPWAO has become an important professional service group for professionals and not just another group of fans with literary pretensions.

One unfortunate side effect for Stearns is that critics claim she has won SPWAO awards for poetry only because of her high profile as a SPWAO activist. This is unfair. Her poetry is certainly as good as any in the field. Other winners in SPWAO's Best Poetry category have not been SPWAO activists or even members when they won the award.

Stearns is a frequent contributor to glossy women's magazines such as *Good Housekeeping, Woman's Day,* and *Family Circle.*

Small-Press Magazine Appearances: *Dragonfields, The Literary Magazine of Fantasy and Terror,* SN
Awards: SPWAO Best Poet, 1980, 1981, 1982

Stevenson, Chris

6892 Marilyn Dr.
Huntington Beach, CA 92687

Stevenson is new to genre poetry. Before writing poetry, Stevenson always viewed it as the work of lazy writers. Since she has turned her hand to poetry, her views have changed. Her work is concerned with conveying a sense of wonder and awe to the reader, always an important concern to science fiction writers. However, it is such a fundamental element in the field that it is not discussed. However for Stevenson, it is the core of her work as a poet.

Commercial Magazine Appearance: AMZ

Stewart, W. Gregory

248 N. Saltair Ave.
Los Angeles, CA 90049

Stewart is emerging as a major figure in science fiction poetry as well as being active in mainstream poetry. His style could be described as light verse, but he uses the form to discuss directly certain universal themes in science fiction, specifically the growing human awareness of our place in the universe. This approach creates a problem: His work may sound pretentious rather than serious to a reader. He generally works his way out of this trap because his language is more complex than that associated with light verse. Stewart does not abjure simple language. He does believe that in many cases the use of simple, clean language does not clarify what the poet is attempting to say to the reader. Its use may simply demean the subject of the poem. His short poems are not constructed as single integrated units, but are a series of smaller units that can stand by themselves as individual poems as well as working together to form a larger one. At present his genre work has appeared only in small-press publications, but it seems likely that his science fiction poems may soon appear in commercial ones. Nevertheless, he does have an appreciative audience for his interesting amalgam of light language and profound themes. His winning the 1987 Rhysling for Long Poem is proof of that.

Small-Press Magazine Appearances: OF, SN, *SPWAO Newsletter*, SL

Anthology Appearance: *1987 Rhysling Anthology*

Award: 1987 Rhysling for Long Poem

Stiles, Michael

P. O. Box 15484
Kansas City, MO 64106

Stiles views most science fiction poems as the work of would-be storytellers. His work also tends to be narratives. The bulk of his work is love poems in which the romantic relationship is described in terms of scientific phenomena. While skillfully done, some may find it cloying.

Commercial Magazine Appearance: AMZ
Small-Press Magazine Appearance: SL

Stone Jr., Del

210 Newcastle Dr.
Fort Walton Beach, FL 32548

Stone's poems are short self-contained pieces, exercises that focus on imagery and theme. He does not use poetry as a storytelling device. Oddly enough, while he does have a syndicated humorous newspaper column, humor does not appear in his poetry. This is unusual only because so much science fiction/fantasy/horror poetry tends to be humorous.

Commercial Magazine Appearance: AMZ

Tem, Steve Rasnic

2500 Irving St.
Denver, CO 80211

A prolific writer of genre poetry, Tem has become an equally prolific writer of horror, science fiction, fantasy, and mystery short stories. His poetry has always looked for the secret meanings behind mundane lives and objects. This quest has been particularly pronounced in his horror poetry and prose, though it has appeared in his other genre work.

In the early 1980s he published and edited *Umbral*, a small-press magazine devoted to speculative poetry. The paperbound anthology of speculative poetry that he published in 1981, *The Umbral Anthology of Science Fiction Poetry*, has been the only small-press nominee for the Phillip K. Dick Award for paperback original.

Earlier in his career he wrote as Steve Rasnic. He has been nominated for the Balrog and the Rhysling.

Commercial Magazine Appearances: AMZ, *Fantastic, Fantasy Newsletter*, IASFM

Small-Press Magazine Appearances: AMRA, *Bennington Review, Blue Flight, Pandora, Patchin Review, Portland Review, Space & Time*, SL, *Velocities, Weird Book, Yakima*

Anthology Appearances: BWV, *1981 Rhysling Anthology, 1983 Rhysling Anthology, The Umbral Anthology of Science Fiction Poetry, A Walk in the Dark*

Thomas, D. M.

10 Greyfriars Ave.
Hereford HR4 0BE
ENGLAND

Thomas first came to the notice of science fiction readers when he wrote many poems for *New Worlds* in its last stage as a forum of speculative prose and poetry. Unlike his *New Worlds* colleagues, he initially kept contact with science fiction roots as he explored the mythic elements of science fiction. Several of these were responses to science fiction stories by Ray Bradbury and Arthur C. Clarke. However, his poetry evolved so that while it discussed mythic themes, it left behind their science fiction roots. Additionally, most of his work became concerned with the erotic life of people and the stress that creates. As can be imagined, Thomas's work is not very approachable, though his earlier work did make it into a few paperback anthologies during the 1970s. Much of the poetry that he wrote in *New Worlds* has appeared in his novels (*The White Hotel, Ararat, Swallow*).

Commercial Magazine Appearance: *New Worlds*
Anthology Appearances: HYEH, *The Umbral Anthology of Science Fiction Poetry*
Anthology Written by Writer:
    Selected Poems. New York: Viking Press, 1988.

Tierney, Richard

c/o Arkham House
Sauk City, WI 53583

Tierney is primarily a horror poet. His work came to positive critical attention in the early 1970s with the rise of the horror-oriented small-press magazine. He has had little success in penetrating commercial markets except for an Arkham House collection and some appearances in *Twilight Zone*. His poems are internal work. The characters in them are the victims of terror that may be psychological rather than supernatural in origin. Tierney rarely clarifies what the source of terror is. This aligns his work with contemporary trends in horror prose.

Commercial Magazine Appearance: *Twilight Zone*
Small-Press Magazine Appearances: *The Arkham Collector, Macabre, Nyctalops, Whispers*
Anthology Written by Writer:
    Collected Poems. Sauk City, WI: Arkham House, 1981.

Turner, Frederick

2668 Aster Dr.
Richardson, TX 75081

As a writer, scholar, theorist, academic, and editor, Frederick Turner is one of the most important figures in American poetry. A handful of his poems could be described as science fiction or speculative in nature. Most of these have appeared in mainstream journals such as *Poetry, Moosehead Review,* and *Spectrum.* His importance to genre poetry lies in the fact that he is one of the few poets to have a book-length science fiction poem published by a major imprint. The work was *The New World,* published by Princeton University Press in 1985, about life in the twenty-first century. Previously, the only commercial publication of a book-length science fiction poem was Henry Martinson's *Aniaria* by Avon Books' SF Rediscovery Series, a short-lived trade paperback line devoted to reprinting obscure but critically significant science fiction work. Unfortunately, *The New World* never received the critical attention within the science fiction community that it did in mainstream circles. One problem may be that Princeton University Press did not market the book to the science fiction community. The other is that the book critics and reviewers who work for mass-market and small-press science fiction magazines do not touch poetry. Most seem to have a genuine fear of commenting on it. If poetry is talked about at all, it is merely to note that such-and-such poetry work is in print and where to order it. The few critics who do talk knowledgeably about poetry, such as Gene Van Troyer and Andrew Joron, usually do so within the pages of *Star*Line,* a publication that talks primarily to other poets, not the average reader. This means that poets do not get the critical analysis that may propel their careers. On the other hand, mediocre poets do not receive the negative attention that ends careers. However, this lack of attention to *The New World* has not stopped Turner from working on a new science fiction book-length poem, *Genesis. Genesis* was released by Saybrook Press in late 1988.

Small-Press Magazine Appearances: *Missouri Review, Moosehead Review, Poetry, Spectrum,* SL

Van Pelt, Jim

1261 Bookcliff Ave., #2
Grand Junction, CO 81501

Van Pelt's poems are curious pieces. They tend to start off as light-hearted amusements, then change mood abruptly, and become rather grim sardonic work.

Small-Press Magazine Appearance: SL

Van Troyer, Gene

Ojana 554
Ginowan City
Okinawa-ken 901-22
JAPAN

Van Troyer started his career in the genre as a speculative poet coming from the mainstream markets. However, unlike other speculative poets, Van Troyer has never seemed to acquire a warmth to mitigate the cold and rather impersonal nature of his work. Still his technical skills are strong enough that his work has found an occasional place in commercial markets despite their forbidding quality. During the early 1980s he was the editor of the *Portland Review,* and under his editorship that magazine became an important showcase within the world of American mainstream journals for science fiction poetry.

Small-Press Magazine Appearances: SL, *Velocities*
Anthology Appearances: BWV, *Poly, 1981 Rhysling Anthology, 1982 Rhysling Anthology, 1983 Rhysling Anthology, The Umbral Anthology of Science Fiction Poetry*

Vaughan, Ralph E.

353 Oxford St.
Chula Vista, CA 92011

Like many poets covered in this book, Vaughan's work wanders among all three genres. However, his poems are all characterized by a strong sense of rhythm and a strong evocation of mythic archetypes. Appropriately, many of his poems focus on horses, an animal that always seems to bring out the mythic in writers. Much of his recent work has appeared in *Hoofstrikes,* a commercial magazine dedicated to horses.

His work as publisher-editor is even more significant to the fields of science fiction, fantasy, and horror poetry. His imprint Running Dinosaur Press has published three chapbooks dedicated to different components of the three genres. The first anthology *Lost Lands* was devoted to lost race fiction as well as historical fantasy. *A Walk in the Dark* was concerned with straightforward horror. *Alternate Lives* examined alternate universes. All three anthologies included original work and reprints of earlier poems by H. P. Lovecraft and Edgar Allan

Poe. Poems in *A Walk in the Dark* and *Alternate Lives* were Rhysling nominees.

Commercial Magazine Appearance: *Hoofstrikes*
Small-Press Magazine Appearances: *Apogee, Bloodrake, Infinity Skewed, Space & Time,* SL, *Tales of the Old West, Undinal Songs Zine.*
Anthology Appearances: A&L, *Alternate Lives, Lost Lands, A Walk in the Dark*

Venable, Lyn

1869 La Cassie, #8
Walnut Creek, CA 94596

Venable is a long-time science fiction pro who wrote poetry early in her career and has now started to return to poetry. She uses poetry as polemical pieces to vent her rage and talk directly about issues that she cannot in prose.

Small-Press Magazine Appearances: *Beyond, Avalon, Dark Starr*

Watkins, William Jon

1406 Garven Ave.
Ocean City, NJ 07712

Watkins' career started as a poet writing in the science fiction anthology market. However, his work as a science fiction novelist and short-story writer has apparently drastically reduced his appearances as a poet. Still his poems do occasionally appear. His work is certainly not cheerful either as a prose writer or a poet. They are dim, rather dystopian views on the future of humans.

Commercial Magazine Appearances: IASFM, *New Worlds Quarterly*
Small-Press Magazine Appearance: *Magazine of Speculative Poetry*

West, Charles

102 E. Clinton, Rm. #11
Fresno, CA 93704

A high school English teacher, West usually works in the genre as a speculative poet. His language is harsh and unsparing for the reader. However, West does put in the occasional joke in the midst of a deadly serious poem. This is something not found among most speculative poets.

Commercial Magazine Appearance: IASFM
Small-Press Magazine Appearances: *Egad, Fantasy Review*, SL, *Velocities*

Wiloch, Thomas

43672 Emrich Dr.
Canton, MI 48187

There is a strong mystical bent to Wiloch's poetry. Many of his poems are concerned with individuals who control events in their universe by the power and passion of their dreams. His poems are expressed in the language of magic rather than science. However, logic of the universes he creates in his poems is so strong that there seems to be no clear boundary between magic and science. Stylistically he uses the prose paragraph as his tool.

Wiloch is currently a writer with the Gale Research Company. In the past he was editor of the short-lived small-press magazine *Grimoire.*

Small-Press Magazine Appearances: *Argonaut*, OF, *Pulpsmith*, SL

Winter-Damon, t.

3264 S. Eastview Ave.
Tucson, AZ 85730

Winter-Damon is like David Skov, an incredibly prolific poet whose work fits neatly into the particular requirements in whatever magazine they appear. Certain technical elements appear again and again in his poems. One is a mass of images that shifts from classical allusion to hard science and back to classical. The other is that despite the density of images in his work, the purpose of his poems is not submerged.

Small-Press Magazine Appearances: *Back Brain Recluse, Beyond, Dreams & Nightmares, Fungi,* SN, SL
Anthology Appearances: *1986 Rhysling Anthology, A Walk in the Dark*

Wolfenbarger, Billy

103 E. Hillcrest Dr.
Eugene, OR 97404

Wolfenbarger is one of those prolific writers whose reputation is based entirely on small-press appearances. Known primarily for his horror in prose and poetry, Wolfenbarger was nominated twice for the Rhysling (1981 and 1982) and once for the Balrog. His poems are strong, first-person narratives that talk to the reader about pain and horror that comes from within the writer.

Small-Press Magazine Appearances: *Beyond the Fields We Know, Diversifier, Dragonfields, Grue, Moonbroth, Myrddin, Night Voyages,* SN, *Shadows of,* SL, *Violent Shadows, Whispered Legends*

Yolen, Jane

Box 27
Hatfield, MA 01038

Jane Yolen is a prolific author of numerous young adult and juvenile fantasy and science fiction novels. She has written five volumes of children's poetry that focus on fantasy themes. She frequently uses poetry in her novels as song lyrics, chapter headings, and chants. However, her poems for newsstand magazines and commercial anthologies are particularly important. While many poets write fantasy poetry, few deal with high fantasy as she does. High fantasy deals with mythic themes and ways that those themes reflect the human state in a universe where there is no doubt as to the existence of magic and supernatural forces. Most fantasy poetry tends to be retelling of knight meets dragon and fair damsel, knight slays dragon, and wins damsel. This does not denigrate their work, but they do not go beyond the needs of plotting. Yolen demonstrates the power of myth. Three of her poems have been nominated for the Rhysling.

Commercial Magazine Appearances: *Fantasy Book*, F&SF, IASFM
Small-Press Magazine Appearance: SL
Anthology Appearances: BWV, *1983 Rhysling Anthology, 1986 Rhysling Anthology*
Anthologies Written by the Writer:
Best Witches. New York: Putnam, 1989.
Dinosaur Dances. New York: Putnam, 1990
Dragon Night & Other Lullabies. New York: Methuen, 1980.
How Beastly. New York: William Collings Books, 1980.
Ring of Earth. San Diego, CA: Harcourt Brace Jovanovich, 1986.
Three Bears Rhyme Book. San Diego, CA: Harcourt Brace Jovanovich, 1987.

Young, Ree

Rt. 2, Box 145-A3
Troy, NC 27371

Young, when working in the genres, is primarily a storyteller. Her poems are optimistic, entertaining, and upbeat. Some poets do not get the attention they deserve from critics or readers because a strong, dark negativism runs through their work. With Young the opposite is true. An upbeat and optimistic style can be equally off-putting. It is a shame because her skill as a poet is excellent. A certain bite in her future work may be what is needed to propel her into the ranks of major genre poets.

Small-Press Magazine Appearances: *Dreams & Nightmares*, SL, *Thin Ice, Z Miscellaneous*

Zelazny, Roger

c/o Kirby McCauley, Ltd.
432 Park Ave. South, Suite 1506
New York, NY 10016

Known primarily as a science fiction novelist who incorporates mythic and high fantasy elements in his work, Zelazny has frequently used poetry in his larger prose work. He has also written two volumes of light verse for the specialty publishers. He has always been interested in light verse.

Commercial Magazine Appearances: AMZ, *Ariel*
Anthologies Written by Writer:
  To Spin Is Miracle Cat. Columbia, PA: Underwood Miller, 1981.
  When Pussywillows Last in the Catyard Bloomed. Columbia,
  PA: Norstrilla Press, 1981.

Zolynas, Al

  c/o Ocean View Press
  P. O. Box 4148
  Mountain View, CA 94040

Zolynas is a speculative poet who is not afraid to talk about himself and his needs in a speculative poem. This personal element is often absent from the work of other speculative poets. Frequently, his family roots become a source for his poetry, emphasizing the impact on cultures of science and the hope it holds.

Small-Press Magazine Appearances: *Pacific Review, Plainsong*
Anthology Appearances: BWV, *Poly*
Anthology Written by Writer:
  The New Physics. Middletown, CT: Wesleyan University
  Press, 1979.

Appendix: Awards

Currently there are two major American awards for science fiction: the "Hugos," which are awarded by the membership of the World Science Fiction Convention, and the "Nebulas," which are awarded by the membership of the Science Fiction Writers of America. Fantasy has the "Howard," which is awarded by the membership of the World Fantasy Convention, and horror has the "Stoker," awarded by the Horror Writers of America. None of these awards has a category for poetry, though poems have occasionally been nominated for the Nebula short-story category.

However, there are two specific awards for poetry. One is the Rhysling, awarded by the Science Fiction Poetry Association. This award is divided into long (over fifty lines) and short (under fifty lines) poetry. The poems may be in any genre (science fiction, fantasy, horror) and appear in any market (commercial, small-press, amateur). The other is the Kelly Award of the Small Press Writers and Artists Organization (SPWAO). Despite its general title, SPWAO focuses on genre small-press activities. Its poetry award is for general achievement over the course of the year rather than for a specific work.

In the past there were two other awards for genre poetry. The Balrogs (1978–1984) had a poetry category that was for general achievement. Among its laureates were Ray Bradbury, H. Warner Munn, Fred Mayer, and Ardath Mayhar. The International Clark Ashton Smith Poetry Awards (1978–1985) were given both for general achievement and individual work. Its laureates included Jonathan Bacon, Ray Bradbury, Marion Zimmer Bradley, Joseph Payne Brennan, George Clayton Johnson, Barry King, Ursula K. LeGuin, Fritz Leiber,

Frederick J. Mayer, H. Warner Munn, Donald Sidney-Fryer, and Roy Squires.

The winners of the Rhysling are:

1978 (first year)

Long Poem: "The Computer Iterates the Greater Trumps," Gene Wolfe

Short Poem: 3-way tie

"The Starman," Duane Ackerson

"Corruption of Metals," Sonya Dorman

"Asleep in the Arms of Mother Night," Andrew Joron

1979

Long Poem: "For the Lady of a Physicist," Michael Bishop

Short Poem: 2-way tie

"Fatalities," Duane Ackerson

"Story Books and Treasure Maps," Steve Eng

1980

Long Poem: "The Sonic Flowerfall of Primes," Andrew Joron

Short Poem: 2-way tie

"The Migration of Darkness," Peter Payack

"Encased in the Amber of Eternity," Robert Frazier

1981

Long Poem: "On Science Fiction," Thomas M. Disch

Short Poem: "Meeting Place," Ken Duffin

1982

Long Poem: "The Well of Baln," Ursula K. LeGuin

Short Poem: "On the Speed of Sight," Raymond DiZazzo

1983

Long Poem: "Your Time and You," Adam Cornford

Short Poem: "In Computers," Alan P. Lightman

1984

Long Poem: "Saul's Death," Joe W. Haldeman
Short Poem: "Two Sonnets," Helen Ehrlich

1985

Long Poem: "A Letter from Caroline Herschel," Siv Cedering
Short Poem: "For Spaces Snarled in the Hair of Comets," Bruce
Boston

1986

Long Poem: "Shipwrecked on Destiny Five," Andrew Joron
Short Poem: "The Neighbor's Wife," Susan Palwick

1987

Long Poem: "Daedalus," W. Gregory Stewart
Short Poem: 2-way tie
"A Dream of Heredity," John Calvin Rezmerski
"Before the Big Bang," Jonathan Post

1988

Long Poem: "White Trains," Lucius Shepard
Short Poem: 2-way tie
"Rocky Road to Hoe," Suzette Haden Elgin
"The Nightmare Collector," Bruce Boston

The SPWAO Kelly Award winners were:
1979 — Steve Eng
1980 — Stephanie Stearns
1981 — Stephanie Stearns
1982 — tie, Stephanie Stearns and Leilah Wendell
1983 — Steve Eng
1984 — Janet Fox
1985 — Denise Dumars
1986 — D. M. Vosk
1987 — Bruce Boston

General Index

Poem Title Index

Listed below are all poems of less than book-length mentioned in this volume.

About the Author

SCOTT E. GREEN is a professional science fiction/fantasy poet residing in Manchester, New Hampshire. He is the author of *Baby Sale at the 7-11* and *Private Worlds*. His poetry has appeared in many publications including *Amazing, Space & Time, Star*Line,* and *American Fantasy.*